FINDING
THE FLOW

PATRICK CERRIA

FINDING THE FLOW

HOW **DALCROZE EURHYTHMICS** AND A NEW APPROACH TO MUSIC EDUCATION CAN IMPROVE PUBLIC SCHOOLS

This book is wholly dedicated to my wife and life partner, Laura, who I love more than anything in the world; also to my son Jack, daughter Annie, and our dog, Cookie. I love you. You're my soul and motivation.

I also dedicate this book to every student I've ever worked with.

CONTENTS

ACKNOWLEDGMENTS

This book could not have happened without the following people, and I must thank all of them: Michael Kibler, John Fowler, and Kevin Cammiso at Kibler, Fowler and Cave in Los Angeles, CA. Stephen Neely at Carnegie Mellon University. Bill Bauer, Michael Joviala, and all of my fellow Dalcroze Society of America colleagues and friends. Ruth Alperson, Leslie Upchurch, Lori Belilove, and the immortal Bob Abramson, who have been, and continue to be, amazing teachers in my life. Mike Kowalski, Reed Leibfried, and Melissa McLaughlin for letting me do what I do. ALL of the teachers, aids, paras, and therapists at Union County Educational Services Commission—it's an honor to work with you. Mallory Saks Zipkin, Barrie Schwarz, Jodi Hotra, Randi Zucker, Robin Brouse, Mike Goldstein, and all of the amazingly dedicated people at the JCC of Central New Jersey. Janelle Ings for not only being an amazing teacher, but for helping me grow, and for being a good friend. Todd Doan, whose soul will always be with me. The immortal legend Hilly Kristal, who cemented my commitment to punk-rock ethics. Amanda Petrusich, whose writing on music and American life (and love of nachos) continues to inspire me. My entire immediate and extended family who are some of the funniest people on the planet and bring immense joy to my life. All of my lifelong friends, who (I'm pretty sure) still don't fully understand what I do for a living. And, of course, Laura, Annie, Jack, and Cookie: the loves of my life.

Without all of you, this book doesn't happen. Thank you!!!

INTRODUCTION

Inclusion/Technology/Science/Medicine/
Academic Research/Self-Discovery

I would like to begin this book by stating I believe the American public education system is the best in the world. I see it as a reflection of our society, in that it is culturally, ethnically, economically, and developmentally diverse. Our public education system, like our democracy, is always in a state of change, evolution, or adaptation—and our schools, like our democracy, are based on an idea of inclusion. We educate all of our children regardless of race, creed, color, religion, or ethnicity—as well as ability, disability, and socioeconomic status. It is an open system, and I see this as its biggest strength. Our public schools are great for these reasons—despite the voices of many education reformers and prominent individuals trying to convince us they're a disaster.

This open system—while being a huge strength—is also what makes our schools very complex. The job of American public education is to take all of these incredibly bright, talented, and diverse students and allow them to reach their fullest creative, intellectual, spiritual, and social potential. This is not just the job of the school but of all the elements of society and community that surround our schools.

However, within the last twenty years, our society has gone through massive changes, and these are affecting the way in which our schools have been able to change and adapt. For one thing, there has been a seismic shift in technological advancements. This has impacted every aspect of our lives. Perhaps the most important impact has been on our children's social, emotional, and physical development—as well as the way they learn.

This technological evolution has also caused subsequent shifts in medical and scientific research. Faster and more efficient technology has led to more efficient ways in how data is collected, sorted, and organized. It has also impacted the way we analyze and treat various medical diagnoses—specifically those that affect our children. One shining example of this is autism spectrum disorder (ASD).

At one time, children with an ASD diagnosis were viewed singularly. It was believed they were able to make it only to specific developmental markers. Today—thanks to medical advancements and the development of better therapies—children with ASD not only make it past developmental markers never before imagined, but many now graduate high school, attend college, or are holding down jobs and are functional members of society.

While technology, science, and medicine made this possible, what really made a significant impact was the evolution of special education. I, personally, can't help but flash back to my public school experience of the 1970s/1980s and what "special education" was like back then. It pales in comparison to the comprehensive programs of today. Our improved model of inclusion has allowed students with special needs to flourish.

I have worked extensively with special-needs students, students living in poverty, as well as inner-city kids, and I'm shocked at how our public schools accommodate so many varied populations of students. It is humbling and overwhelming. Mind you, this wasn't always the case. At one time, we did not come close to educating our special-needs children as comprehensively as we do now. In fact, we practically barred them from public schools all together. But that changed and evolved over time.

Is our system perfect? No, but our schools will continue to evolve, change, and adapt, because they always do.

I believe we've reached the next big point of change regarding our schools and overall education system. These pages are an attempt to point out what I see as some obvious evolutions and adaptations that need to occur. I don't believe the system is broken. Rather, I think we need to step back and reexamine how we're teaching our kids and—more importantly—how we're training our teachers. It's time to make some adjustments.

This book is the result of all of my experiences teaching and working with students of varied ages, backgrounds, and abilities. I have been lucky enough to teach in schools that serve inner-city children; physically disabled students; developmentally disabled students; students who have behavioral and emotional classifications; students classified as at-risk; and those who are typically developing.

I have worked with students as young as eighteen months all the way through to twenty-one years. I have taught students who were nonverbal, and I've taught students who were on probation after being arrested. I've worked with students who were contemplating joining a gang, and I've worked with those who were heartbroken because they didn't make their high school golf team. I am proud to say that I have worked with an array of wonderful kids.

In addition to my teaching experience, this book is also inspired by my studies in a method of teaching music called Dalcroze Eurhythmics. I completed a three-year study in Eurhythmics and was awarded an Elementary Teaching Certificate from The Juilliard School in Manhattan. Since that completion, I've worked with all of the aforementioned populations of kids and have been humbled by what Eurhythmics enables me to do as a teacher. As of the writing of this book, I am in the next phase of Eurhythmics studies at the Marta Sanchez Dalcroze Training Center at Carnegie Mellon University in Pittsburgh, Pennsylvania.

Around three years ago, I decided to begin going into public schools to present staff-development workshops on Eurhythmics. Initially, I went and spoke solely to music educators. As time went on, I found myself speaking to more and more *non*-music educators. Classroom teachers began coming to my workshops to hear about Eurhythmics-based strategies for their students.

After a couple of years of presenting my workshops, I was invited to speak at an early-childhood-educator conference in Chicago, where I spoke to more than 300 teachers, none of whom were music educators.

The message I was hearing from both classroom and music educators was loud and clear: Their students were more socially and developmentally diverse, and this was making their job more complex. In addition to this was the sudden view of education—and learning—as a global contest. Teachers were telling me how they were now responsible for teaching subjects at breakneck speed to roomfuls of developmentally and socially diverse students and that this was affecting the entire class dynamic.

Of all the skills teachers must possess, classroom management has become the toughest to maintain. Creating a healthy classroom dynamic has become more and more difficult, for a number of reasons. I believe what is further complicating effective classroom-management skills is that teachers are not being adequately trained to face the varied populations of students they must now teach. They walk into classrooms and are, literally, overwhelmed.

As I was getting ready to complete this book, something else happened that had a profound effect not just on education but on life as a whole: The COVID-19 pandemic. Everything about school, education, life, society, and economics was essentially thrown out the window.

America was suddenly confronted by the extended role "school" plays in our lives. It turns out it's not just the building where our children go to learn math, science, and reading. It's also the place where many kids get their breakfast and lunch, where others receive structure, discipline, and guidance, and make lifelong friendships. Perhaps the most shocking thing that emerged was just how important school is to the daily functionality of society. It turns out that our schools are essential parts of our communities in ways we were never made to see before.

In addition, the role of technology in education suddenly experienced a massive shift. Public school districts across the United States moved to remote and virtual models of teaching. Educators who had been teaching live in a classroom for thirty years were suddenly told they'd be teaching through applications with names like Zoom and Google Meet.

Teachers across the country were asked to make a never imagined pivot in how they teach, and what their idea of a classroom was. Classroom management became an even more complex task as it now had to be done within the context of a what amounted to a live group video chat.

As the 2019/2020 schoolyear ended, rituals and rites of passage that are as much a part of education as academics were completely derailed. Senior proms as well as middle and high school graduation ceremonies were cancelled. As summer began, it was assumed that by the fall we would be able to go back to something resembling "normal" school. This was not the case.

As I am writing this, there are students across the US who have not set foot inside their school for over a year. There are students who started their freshman year of high school remotely. I personally teach students who are stressed out by the whole thing. Likewise I have students who have rolled with it and haven't been affected at all.

The COVID-19 pandemic has shown us that—by and large—technology cannot replace what in-person education provides for most of our kids. Education is complex and the pandemic has shed light on a fact that most every educator and parent understands: Not every child learns the same way.

In the following pages, I try to address not only the changes that have affected our schools but also what I believe we can do to help move them in the right direction. I used not only my own experience as inspiration but also the voices of the hundreds of teachers I've worked with over the years. In addition, this book is a direct result of the thousands of students I have taught and continue to teach. They are, after all, the reason I do what I do.

I see education as a journey of self-discovery. It is something that involves not only learning but also trust, as well as emotional, social, and physical growth, along with curiosity, discovery, and, most of all, guidance.

As teachers, we have to simultaneously be able to do all of those things—in addition to teaching our subject(s). I hope this book can help with that.

1
DEVELOPMENTAL DIVERSITY

*Technological, Scientific, and Medical Advances/Individuals
With Disabilities Education Act/Inclusive Schools*

This may sound crazy, but I'm going to begin a book about how I believe music education can improve public education by writing about advances in computer technology. I ask that you bear with me.

We now take computers and other digital technologies for granted. They have become a regular part of our lives. They not only provide communication services (email, text, video chat, phone calls) but are also where we do a majority of our written work—be it math related and/or research. In addition, they now provide hours of entertainment.

We watch movies and TV shows not only on our computers but also on our phones and tablets. We can live-stream sporting events anywhere, anytime. Streaming—as it's now known—has become a huge part of society, so much so that the phrase "binge watch" is now part of the cultural lexicon.

Computers also do things like start our cars in the morning, turn our house alarms on or off, store our music and photograph files, host websites like Amazon, track the packages we ordered from Amazon, enable us to balance our bank accounts from the living-room sofa, make our plane and hotel reservations, and even read the paper.

What many of us don't realize is that the computer has been evolving since the 1940s. Starting with the Z3—built in Germany in 1941—we have experienced a never-ending digital evolution. While the early computer's primary concern was helping to solve math problems or crack codes (like the British Bombe, designed by Alan Turing to help break the German "Enigma" code during WWII), evolutions have since allowed them to handle data crunching as well as all of the aforementioned entertainment outlets.

In addition to its physical design, the other evolution in computers has been the speeds at which they process information. We have all seen photographs of early computers that occupied entire rooms. Our modern-day models not only fit in our pockets but process information at blazing speeds—and this is only going to increase.

In addition to processing information fast, computers also organize and sort it for us. The sorted and organized data that comes out of our machines has affected many facets of our lives. One example is how modern statistical analysis has impacted the game of baseball. Teams now base pitching changes, batting lineups, and entire game strategies on computer-generated data they've accumulated on opposing teams, as well as individual players. Because the manager in the dugout has well-researched and sorted data on every batter, he can shift his defense based on where he knows each batter will most likely hit the ball. If he has a lefty pitcher in the midst of a close game, and his data tells him the next batter due up hits lefties really well, he'll take that pitcher out and put in a righty. Computer-generated data has, literally, changed the sport.

When you're going on a long trip, or even around the corner, you now enter your destination into an application on your phone. Not only will the application tell you how to reach your destination but will also alert you to shorter routes *as you're driving.* Your phone is actually processing and analyzing live data regarding traffic patterns, accidents, and/or construction—and doing so at lightning speed.

What began with the Z3 evolved over the last sixty years and has dramatically shifted our lives. One area that has seen the fruits of this evolution is medicine—and one of the biggest pushes behind this was the Human Genome Project (HGP).

The HGP was created to map out the genetic structure of human cells so that scientists could better explore what we all have in common. The idea for the HGP began in 1984 but did not go into full effect until 1990. Taking advantage of existing digital technology, the HGP team began developing technologies of their own. These were aimed at developing advanced techniques that could help analyze and further study the role human DNA has in disease. A secondary objective was to see how illness specifically affects our physiology.

In 1996, the HGP sponsored a summit meeting in Bermuda. At this summit, it was agreed that:

". . . all human genomic sequence information
generated by centers for large-scale human sequencing
should be made freely available and in the public
domain within 24 hours after generation."[1]

Essentially, the HGP wanted to create a massive database. This could then be used openly by the medical, academic, and scientific communities to exchange ideas, reference information, and see what other people had discovered. These became known as the Bermuda Principles and were like a worldwide interactive database. It was, essentially, crowd-sourced science . . . by scientists. This changed the existing idea of research—which was generally saved for publication in medical journals—and made it more of an open source for scientists from around the world. Again, technology was at its root.

The byproducts of the HGP were almost immediate. In 1999—only three years after the Bermuda Principles—scientists were able to sequence human Chromosome 22. This was the most continuous piece of DNA ever decoded. Scientists could now get a look into how disease and illness affected cell structure. It also allowed for scientists and medical professionals to develop new approaches and techniques for treatment. The amazing thing is that the Chromosome

---

1 "A Brief History of the Human Genome Project" Website: https://unlockinglifescode.org/timeline?tid=4

22 research was a result of scientists collaborating from the US, England, Japan, France, Germany, and China. The open source of the HGP was already producing results.

The byproduct was that, throughout the 1990s and beyond, medical research took on a whole new life. The world experienced the benefits of this regarding the COVID-19 pandemic. When the virus was discovered in China, scientists immediately ran the viral DNA code through a supercomputer to get a detailed breakdown of the virus and its unique spike protein. The information that the computer provided became the blueprint for the vaccines that emerged less than a year later.

One area that has benefitted tremendously was the way we diagnose and treat children with physical disabilities as well as those with developmental and sensory-based delays.

As technology allowed for better insight into the causes of developmental disabilities, improvements in various treatments and therapies made them more effective and sped up their development. This had an incredible impact not just for children with disabilities but also for their parents. Breakthroughs in protocols such as occupational and physical therapy allowed children to develop past physical points and developmental markers in a way never thought possible.

Further developments in specific therapies, such as Applied Behavior Analysis (ABA), allowed evolutions in the treatment of children on the Autism spectrum and with other sensory-based delays. Speech therapies also improved and allowed professionals to discover that many subsequent behavioral problems associated with sensory-based delays were rooted in the frustration of children not being able to communicate and express themselves.

Because of the HGP, breakthroughs in the science of genetics led to earlier diagnosis and improved treatment. All of this demanded evolutionary change in the mindset in not only how children with special needs were treated but also in how they could be educated.

The history of special education in the United States is complicated. We, as a nation, have always flirted with denial when it
comes to how we educate students with special needs. This, unfortunately, is still the case. As recently as 2017, the state of Texas got
into a lot of trouble for the way they treated students who were
legally entitled to receive special-education services. According to
a report in the *Houston Chronicle*, the state systematically denied
services to ". . . tens of thousands of families . . ." Why did the
Texas Education Agency do this? To put it simply: money. What
happened in Texas shows how special education is still a difficult
and sore subject within our public education system, despite the
evolution of special-education policies over time.

In 1975, the United States passed a piece of landmark legislation
called the Education for All Handicapped Children Act (EAHCA), but
the passing of EAHCA was the result of a long and difficult journey.

Before 1975, children with varying disabilities and/or diagnoses
were literally excluded from their public schools. Many states went so
far as to enact laws flat out barring children from their schools who
were blind, deaf, or suffered emotional or developmental disabilities.
According to the Department of Education, in 1970, American public schools educated only one in every five children with disabilities.
EAHCA was vital because it meant that some—but not all—special-
needs children would now have access to their public school.

EAHCA was more than a response to a need to educate disabled
children. It was a byproduct of other things that had been building
for more than twenty years. These included programs such as the
Training of Professional Personnel Act (1959) and the Teachers of the
Deaf Act (1961). These programs trained educators to accommodate
varied learners. They also woke people up to the fact that disabled
children oftentimes were more intelligent than initially thought. This
helped to slowly break the practice of placing young children and

high-school-aged kids into mental hospitals, where they were mistreated or ignored. This also slowly helped to discover that—through use of proper techniques—disabled children could actually be taught in a proper school environment. By 1968, more than 30,000 special-education teachers were working in public schools, thanks to federally funded programs.

The 1972 federal ruling *Mills v. Board of Education of the District of Columbia* mandated that all states educate children with disabilities. The education of disabled children was now covered in the Equal-Protection clause of the 14th Amendment to the Constitution. *Mills* also mandated that districts could not use excuses such as poor funding or lack of administration to deny education to disabled students.

Mills helped special education evolve further and served as an early sign of things to come. Still, many districts put only small or ineffective programming in place, and children were still underserved or ignored by their public school districts. When EAHCA was passed, it helped further the development of programming that *Mills* mandated.

As EAHCA and its policies settled into the public-school landscape, technological and medical evolutions were beginning to pick up speed. The '70s and '80s saw massive technological jumps, and, by the time the '90s rolled around, the HGP was in full swing. The snowball of research, technology, and scientific/medical collaboration was reaching a pinnacle. This also led to improved therapy techniques, which allowed for growth and development in special-needs kids previously thought impossible. This prompted the asking of a significant question regarding our special-needs children: If improved therapies could progress children's development up to, and past, certain points, why not make therapies a part of the education process?

In 1997, EAHCA was amended and became the Individuals with Disabilities Education Act (IDEA). This further ensured that children with disabilities were entitled to a free public education.

One of, if not the, most significant thing that IDEA did was state that special-needs students were now entitled to the *individual* services that came with that education. This language helped to implement early-intervention programs into public education as well as things like Individualized Education Programs (IEPs), amounting to a paradigm shift in American public education that we are still adjusting to and coming to terms with.

According to the National Center for Educational Statistics, 14% of the American public-school population now receives special-education services—that's 7.1 million children nationwide. To put that in perspective for you, the overall population of the state of Rhode Island is 1.1 million people. That means seven Rhode Islands solely populated with special-needs kids report to public schools every day, and these children come with an array of diagnoses and classifications.

Advances in medicine have also provided the ability to zero in on statistics relative to specific disorders affecting our kids. These statistics and data show just how developmentally diverse our children are. An important study done by the Centers for Disease Control and Prevention (CDC) on neurological-based disabilities in American children ages 3 to 17 produced some staggering statistics:

- 3.2% have a diagnosis of depression (approximately 1.9 million)
- 7.1% have a diagnosis of anxiety (approximately 4.4 million)
- 7.4% have a diagnosed behavioral classification (approximately 4.5 million)
- 9.4% (children aged 2–17 years) have a diagnosis of Attention Deficit Hyperactivity Disorder (approximately 6.1 million)[2]

2 "Data and Statistics on Children's Mental Health" Centers for Disease Control and Prevention Website: https://www.cdc.gov/childrensmentalhealth/data.html

What's amazing to me about that study is the significant number of children diagnosed with something as serious as depression. Yet, diagnoses in other neurological disabilities *increase* beyond that. It's also important to note that these statistics are pre-COVID-19 pandemic. This is how the American public-school classroom looks today.

Science and technology are providing us with more insight into the developmental diversity of our students. This has meant dramatic change in all aspects of education. School faculties have changed and now include in-class aides, paraprofessionals, and occupational (OT), physical (PT), and speech therapists—in addition to teachers. Many districts now offer extended-school-year programs, specifically for children on the Autism spectrum. These require the hiring of full-time summer staff or paying full-time staff to remain on through the month of July.[3]

This has also meant physical change to school buildings themselves. Districts have dedicated whole classrooms, corridors, or, in many cases, entire buildings to accommodate special-needs populations. School-based early-intervention programs begin providing services to children as young as three years, further increasing the need for classrooms, physical space, and staff.

Modern public school administrations now include—in addition to Principals and Vice Principals—entire child-study teams composed of psychiatrists and/or behavioral specialists. They oversee the development of protocols like Individualized Education Programs and behavioral modification programs—which have become standard pieces of public education. These protocols require detailed communication between the child study teams, parents, principals, and medical professionals. Administrators must also communicate with teachers, aides, and therapists. As therapies and treatments evolve, so must the school's policies and protocols.

---

3 My district's extended school year now runs into early August.

Thanks to IDEA, we've come to realize that educating children with special needs is nothing short of dynamic. Walk into any American public school, and you will find a developmentally diverse space that includes students who have not only physical disabilities but also sensory and/or developmental delays. There may also be students with behavioral and emotional classifications. Within a single classroom, it is not unusual to find three varied learning types and/ or multiple aides or paraprofessionals. Students leave at various points for therapies and/or "pull-outs," in which they receive one-on-one or small-class instruction in specific subjects. Teachers, therapists, aides, parents, and the Child Study Team all work together to make sure needs are met and progress is being made. It is extraordinary, and it has served to show us that the education of <u>all</u> children is incredibly complex—not just for those with special needs.

American public schools are now more inclusive than they've ever been. They—like our country—are more diverse, which means that teaching, which has always been a dynamic and creative profession, has become even more so. I think it's important to repeat this: *Teaching, which has always been a dynamic and creative profession, has become even more so.*

These varied and dynamic populations are what American teachers are facing when they walk into their classroom, and these same populations are what faced school districts across the nation as they closed due to COVID-19. This developmental diversity within our schools is but one piece affecting the way we teach our kids. Developmental diversity is not a singular element but part of a much-larger picture.

2

THE SOCIAL, EMOTIONAL, AND DEVELOPMENTAL EFFECTS OF TECHNOLOGY AND CHILDHOOD POVERTY

Sense of Self/Social Media/Extrinsic vs. Intrinsic/Outdoor Play/Human Interaction/Empathy/Childhood Poverty

In *Hamlet*, Shakespeare has the character Polonius speak these immortal words to his son, Laertes:

"This above all: to thine own self be true."

These words are now often found hanging on classroom walls, written on refrigerator magnets, or even on Facebook posts. Maybe they're among some of the most overused Shakespearean words. I believe they're vital when it comes to what is happening with our kids today.

When we think of education, we immediately think of academic subjects like math, science, writing, reading, etc. One thing not considered enough is how education develops us *within*—how, beginning that first day of kindergarten or pre-school, we begin interacting with peers, exploring new ideas, and hearing other people's perspectives.

We see, meet, and interact with other students who may not look like us and maybe dress differently than we do. Perhaps they talk differently, too. We are suddenly thrust into a whole new social environment where change is both a curiosity and a challenge. The term "peer pressure" exists for a reason. How much of those around us do we want to emulate? How much do we ignore? School is a place for not only academic growth and development but also for social, emotional, and creative growth.

Academic development makes this process more complex as it provides further questions toward a student's developing sense of self. Students not only learn new subjects but begin to consider how they apply personally. As students progress through school, these considerations become deeper questions: *What subjects do I like? What am I good at? What interests me? Can I make a living doing it?* Compounding these questions is social and emotional development, as well as peer pressure: *Who do I want to be? What kind of person am I? How do I see myself?* These are commonly known as "inner skills," and the formation of healthy inner skills is essential to the overall development of our kids.

Young people have always been affected by those around them. However, the difference between, say, middle-school students in the 1950s, '60s, and '70s, and middle-school students today is that those from the past left school, and, for the most part, the peer and social pressures stayed there, too. They got home from school, had a snack, and went outside to play. Maybe they went upstairs to read a book. Perhaps they read a magazine or listened to the radio. If they watched TV, it meant a selection of maybe five channels.

Today, a typical middle-school student leaves school and, as she's walking out the door, pulls out her phone to check social media. Some of her classmates have already posted photos of themselves walking home together. Based on the photos, it's the *craziest* and *best walk home from school ever*. By the time she gets home, that same group has posted another update, or video, of them having something to eat at a local pizza place. Maybe they posted a group TikTok. *Why wasn't I invited?* she thinks as she's staring into her phone.

As she puts her phone down, it buzzes: it's a text from a friend asking if she's seen the images and videos the other group have been posting. In a series of text messages (not face-to-face or live conversation), the two friends commiserate and/or speculate as to why they were left out of the outing.

As the text-message discussion ends, her phone buzzes again: another photo update. As she scrolls past it, there's an ad for one of her favorite clothing stores. She clicks through and notices the ad features a shirt one of the girls in the photo from the pizzeria was wearing. She wonders if she can afford the shirt—and begins to wonder if her sense of style is why she wasn't asked to join the group for pizza.

By this time, forty-five minutes has passed, and the girl has not stopped interacting with her phone. In that time, she's questioned herself not from within but based on what's transpired on the screen of an electronic device. She has been bombarded with information and this has taken place while she is all alone. She has *interacted* with others, but not physically, emotionally, or in person. She has looked into other people's lives and drawn conclusions—again, not through live interaction.

She has also been inundated with advertisements that were, themselves, generated by artificial intelligence. The music she listens to comes from a streaming service and, based on her selections and/or playlists, provides other musical suggestions with a caption that maybe says *"Because you liked . . ."*

The girl toggles between social media applications (TikTok, Instagram, Snapchat) while checking Twitter. Her music is still going. It is a non-stop stream of sounds, images, people, places, and impressions. It's important to remember that, throughout this experience, she is alone.

In 2012 something very important happened in our society: the percentage of Americans who own smartphones surpassed 50 percent. Social media and smartphone technology have drastically changed the way our children begin to perceive who they are. The natural questions they ask of themselves regarding self-discovery have been corrupted.

Klaus Schwab, the founder and executive director of the World Economic Forum, believes that we are living in the Fourth Industrial Revolution. As Mr. Schwab has cited, the First Industrial Revolution was the result of humans discovering the power of steam and water. The second was further harnessing the power of electricity. The third was about electronic-based information technology. This current revolution is unique, Schwab believes, because it is not solely based on a power source. This revolution is about a fusion of technologies that is blurring the lines between the digital, physical, and biological.

Technology is now crossing all kinds of lines and is doing so at a rate of speed and development that is unprecedented. The result is that our lives have been profoundly affected, and not just from the perspective of commerce. This revolution has caused us to question things such as:

- Self-Identity
- Ownership
- Consumption patterns
- The separation of work and leisure
- Skill sets
- Human interaction and relationships

Mr. Schwab commented on the effects of this and said something that simultaneously intrigued me and gave me chills:

"One of the features of this fourth industrial revolution is that it doesn't change what we are doing, but it changes us."

There are many child psychologists who believe one of the most significant changes we've seen in our kids is a shift from *intrinsic* to *extrinsic* thinking. Intrinsic thinking is creating our own ideas and philosophies from within. It's processing information and then coming up with personal goals and plans based on who you believe yourself to be. This belief is based on a deep dive within your own thoughts, ideas, human interactions, and perception of those things around you.

Extrinsic thinking is the opposite. It is the creation of goals based on what *other* people may think. This way of thinking is motivated by materialistic pursuits—being rich, social status, and/or being "good looking." This thinking may cause friction with the real person one knows themself to be inside. It clashes with the intrinsic and can result in stress, depression, and anxiety.

Kids are now growing up in a world where likes, followers, and views carry social status and self-acceptance. These are garnered through photos or images posted to social media and typically are based on how one looks, who they're with, and where they're at. The likes, views, and followers come twenty-four hours a day, seven days a week. Young people are constantly searching for peer validation, and the added stress of how many likes and followers one has can lead to self-doubt and a feeling of vulnerability. This has impacted the way our kids think as well as their social and emotional intelligence—and these ultimately affect their mindset when they come to school.

As smartphone use increased among kids, so did diagnoses of anxiety and depression. Some child psychologists have referred to this as "Duck Syndrome"—meaning that, as young people try harder and harder for peer validation, they duck deeper into their phones.

Dr. Jean Twenge is a psychologist who has written extensively on generational differences. She refers to the current generation (born between 1995 and 2012) as "iGen." They are unique in that they have grown up not knowing what life is like without Internet and/or smartphone technology.

Twinge wrote an article for *The Atlantic* that carried the ominous title: "Have Smartphones Destroyed a Generation?" The article discusses the effects of social media on our kids.

I have seen these effects firsthand. The way our kids socialize and the way they think have been drastically impacted. I have two children of my own, so I look at this technological advance from the perspectives of both a parent and an educator. It's incredible to see how technology has changed not only the way our kids communicate but also the way they study for tests, arrange practices for sports teams, obtain news and cultural information, and plan their social lives.

But this technology has also impacted the way they (and we) think. The phone is no longer just a tool used to communicate. It is now the way kids—literally—do everything. It's how many kids read books or articles. It's how they watch movies and listen to music. For some, it's how they do *all* of those things *at the same time*. It is information overload, and to think this isn't affecting the way our children's minds process information is shortsighted.

Digital technologies like smartphones and/or tablets provide students with access to an endless supply of valuable materials. The Internet is, indeed, a world of limitless sources and information, but are we teaching our kids to use it like that? I remember when the Internet was brand new and was labeled the "information superhighway"—and while things like the HGP have proven that label true, there seem to be more websites and smartphone applications whose purpose is not to provide facts and information but, rather, to do the complete opposite.

The question "What is truth?" needs to be asked today. It is no secret that, in our current society, the idea and concept of truth is in jeopardy. Students can go onto websites, or their Twitter feed, and discover 16 different stories revolving around a singular event. Conspiracy theories that were once limited to the fringe of society or the front pages of supermarket tabloids are suddenly mainstream narratives. Truth, and how to find it, now needs to be something taught in our schools—and this is also adding to the pressure of self-discovery.

The Internet and smartphone applications provide immediate access to an unprecedented amount of entertainment and information. It's like having a semi-truck filled with vinyl records drive up to your house every day and empty its contents into your front yard. Right behind it is a semi-truck filled with books, then one with newspapers, then another with movies and videos. That, literally, happens every day. How much of that information are kids, and adults, taking in? How much are we actually processing? How much are we retaining? How much of it is true?

Technology has advanced, and young people have the world, literally, in the palm of their hand. The problem is, when young people read off of these devices, it's the equivalent of skimming across the surface of a lake on a jet ski. Trees fly by, as do other jet skiers and boats. There are loud sounds and water splashing into your face. It's distracting and difficult to concentrate.

In addition to the increasing effects of technology on typically developing kids, teachers are also dealing with the aforementioned populations of special-needs students in school. In many instances, students suffering at the hands of technology do not have a formal classification or diagnosis, thus making a teacher's job even more complex.

As students spend more time on phones or with other technologies, another area of growth and development that suffers is outdoor play. It is not a secret that kids do not play outside as much as they used to, and the decline in outdoor play is not new. It's been happening for a while now.

It is important to view the benefits of outdoor play not only through the lens of our own childhood but also for the social and developmental benefits. Running around outside does more than just expose kids to fresh air. It engulfs them in the world of nature and all of its stimulation. Walking barefoot in the grass on a July day is not just about being carefree but is also an exercise in sensory stimulation: We feel the different blades of grass and their textures pushing into our soles. The nerves in our feet pick up on the unevenness of the ground and cause us to use our balance. We may feel a sudden temperature change as we cross a patch of cool mud or dirt. Perhaps you accidentally step on a bee, pine cone, or other sharp object. Maybe you decide to walk on tiptoes at some point, forcing yourself to use another type of balance.

The joy of swinging on a swing and feeling yourself fly through the air provides hours of outdoor fun. But this activity, too, is an exercise in sensory stimulation and input. Pumping your legs in an effort to go higher teaches weight distribution and body awareness. Using your arms and hands to pull the chains back as you move forward teaches you to use balance and gross motor function. Watching the horizon move up and down with the rhythm of your motion gives you a different perspective on your surroundings. Maybe, at some point, you jumped off the swing. Not only did you enjoy a moment of free fall, but then you had to land and, again, use your balance.

The great writer Paul Auster authored a book titled *Winter Journal*, which is the story of his own social and emotional development told from the perspective of his body. This passage, I believe, speaks to the power and importance of outdoor play:

"What presses on in you, what has always pressed on in you: the outside, meaning the air—or more precisely, your body in the air around you. The soles of your feet anchored to the ground, but all the rest of you exposed to the air, and that is where the story begins, in your body . . ."

Playing outside—while being fun—is essential to our development. It helps create who we become inside.

Outdoor play is also essential to the development of the vestibular nervous system. The vestibular nerves are located within our ears, which each contain three circular canals. These canals are filled with a fluid called *endolymph*. When we move our heads, the endolymph shifts inside of the canals. This movement is picked up by receptors inside the canals and sends messages to our brains about our body movements and direction. This function is essential to our sense of balance as well as our coordinated movements.

Our vestibular system—along with our eyes, muscles, joints, sense of touch, and even sense of smell—is responsible for our overall sense of balance and movement. If we aren't using it, our sense of balance and overall body awareness suffers. The vestibular system is a significant piece of our physiology. If it is not stimulated and developed properly, it ultimately affects our physical development. Imagine how students who don't get enough vestibular stimulation come into the classroom and learn.

According to data from the CDC, the diagnosis rate of ADHD among kids ages 3–17 was 7.8% in 2003. That number climbed to 9.5% in 2007 and then climbed again in 2011 to 11%. A 2014 *Washington Post* article titled "Why So Many Kids Can't Sit Still in Class Today" had pediatric occupational therapist Angela Hanscom addressing her beliefs as to why:

"The problem: children are constantly in an upright position these days. It is rare to find children rolling down hills, climbing trees, and spinning in circles just for fun. Merry-go-rounds and teeter-totters are a thing of the past. Recess times have shortened due

to increasing educational demands, and children rarely play outdoors due to parental fears, liability issues, and the hectic schedules of modern-day society. Let's face it: Children are not nearly moving enough, and it is really starting to become a problem."

She continues:

"I recently observed a fifth-grade classroom as a favor to a teacher. I quietly went in and took a seat toward the back of the classroom. The teacher was reading a book to the children, and it was toward the end of the day. I've never seen anything like it. Kids were tilting back in their chairs at extreme angles, others were rocking their bodies back and forth, a few were chewing the ends of their pencils, and one child was hitting a water bottle against his forehead in a rhythmic pattern.

"This was not a special-needs classroom but a typical classroom at a popular art-integrated charter school. My first thought was that the children might have been fidgeting because it was the end of the day and they were simply tired. Even though this may have been part of the problem, there was certainly another underlying reason.

"We quickly learned, after further testing, that most of the children in the classroom had poor core strength and balance. In fact, we tested a few other classrooms and found that, when compared to children from the early 1980s, only <u>one out of twelve children had normal strength and balance</u> [my emphasis]. <u>Only one!</u> [my emphasis]"

Hanscom then goes on to write about the importance of developing the vestibular system. This is done through hours of movement and free play. If kids are not engaging in this type of activity, their systems are not developing properly. How does this correlate to learning? Hanscom one more time:

> *"Children are going to class with bodies that are less prepared to learn than ever before. With sensory systems not quite working right, they are asked to sit and pay attention. Children naturally start fidgeting in order to get the movement their body so desperately needs and is not getting enough of to 'turn their brain on' . . . fidgeting is a real problem. It is a strong indicator that children are not getting enough movement throughout the day."*

An underdeveloped sensory system translates into kids who cannot sit still in school—yet another challenge presented to teachers. And, as noted above, this problem is not limited to public schools. Kids with underdeveloped sensory systems not only suffer decreased balance and attention spans, but they're also more likely to act out in class and present behavioral problems.

These could lead to subsequent anxiety issues. Poor core strength also leads to weight gain and possible obesity. What has our solution been? When our kids get to school, the first thing we tell them to do is *sit down*, and, in most cases, they sit there for the next two to three *hours*.

If kids are coming to school and feel they do not have control over their bodies or are under-stimulated physically, how can we expect them to learn? Our kids are becoming more detached not only from their natural surroundings but also from each other. Playing less outside in a free, open environment (not a scheduled "playdate") has vast impacts. We're not giving kids time to explore or be together in a free and open space. This is essential to their development.

In his 2005 book *Last Child in the Woods: Saving Our Kids from Nature Deficit Disorder*, Richard Louv writes extensively on why our kids need to be outside. One thing I learned from his book that I didn't know before is that "nature smart" is an actual form of intelligence included in the list of multiple intelligences. This list was created by Harvard University professor of education Howard Gardner, who, in 1983, developed the theory of multiple intelligence. Up until Gardner, a child's intelligence was solely based on an IQ Test score. Thankfully, Gardner viewed this as much too limited and devised his theory. Initially there were only seven intelligences listed (I am using the order that Louv used in his book):

- Linguistic Intelligence (word smart)
- Logical Mathematical Intelligence (number/reasoning smart)
- Spatial Intelligence (picture smart)
- Bodily/Kinesthetic Intelligence (body smart)
- Musical Intelligence (music smart)
- Interpersonal Intelligence (people smart)
- Intrapersonal Intelligence (self-smart)

At some point, in the evolution of his theory, Gardner added the "eighth intelligence" to his list: Naturalist Intelligence (nature smart). He did this because he realized how important our connection to nature and the world around us is. It's not only about books and study time. Spending time outside and "reading" the natural world around us is an essential piece to our development of understanding and of discovery. If we continue to allow our kids to be over-scheduled or define "play" as video games or two hours of soccer practice a week, we're just hurting them even more. Here's Louv on how modern life has affected outdoor play:

"It takes time—loose, unstructured dreamtime—to experience nature in a meaningful way. Unless parents are vigilant, such time becomes a scarce resource, not because they intend it to shrink, but because time is consumed by multiple, invisible forces; because our culture places so little value on natural play."[4]

There is such alarm about the lack of free play amongst our children that the American Academy of Pediatrics (AAP) recently issued a report stating that, as part of "well visits" for children, pediatricians should prescribe play. That's right: it's gotten so bad that medical professionals have intervened and are now writing prescriptions for outdoor play[5]. Why? The report from the AAP states:

"Play is not frivolous: it enhances brain structure and function and promotes executive function (i.e., the

---

4 *Last Child in the Woods: Saving Our Children from Nature Deficit Disorder*, by Richard Louv, pp 117–118

5 !

process of learning, rather than the content), which allows us to pursue goals and ignore distractions." [6]

Our sensory systems are vital not only to our physiological development but also to our neurological, social, and emotional development. It also helps to create and develop a sense of self. Everything we experience—see, hear, touch, taste, smell—is passed through our sensory system, and our responses to these are ultimately shaped by emotions. To think that sensory development is not vital to the way kids learn is shortsighted. Not allowing kids the time to develop these senses is an affront to childhood development, learning, and education as a whole.

As our kids seemingly grow less attached to the world around them and to each other, something else has begun to happen: a decline in empathy and understanding of others. The world that exists within screens lacks emotion. Kids can call each other names or make comments without consideration of emotional response. You can't read the facial expression of the person you just called a "jerk" on Twitter. Spend a few minutes on a friend's Facebook feed and read how people now "speak" to each other. There's even a name for this: trolling [7].

A recent study done at the University of Michigan reported a 48% decrease in empathy among college students. Can you imagine if there were a 48% decrease in college-student math scores? The

---

6 From the August 2018 American Academy of Pediatrics Clinical Report "The Power of Play: A Pediatric Role in Enhancing Development in Young Children," by Michael Yogman, Andrew Garner, Jeffrey Hutchinson, Kathy Hirsh-Pasek, Roberta Michnik Golinkoff, Committee on Psychosocial Aspects of Child and Family Health, Council on Communications and Media

7 Full disclosure: I quit Facebook more than four years ago. I, personally, couldn't take what it was doing to many friends and family members. Right before my eyes, they were morphing into loudmouthed, inconsiderate yahoos.

same study also reported a 34% decrease in college students' ability to respect other people's perspectives. Add to this our increased detachment from the outdoors, and you begin to grasp the severity of what's happening with our kids today.

The students coming into our classrooms are dynamic and diverse in ways we have never considered. The bigger question is, "How are teachers supposed to teach these children?" Are we training teachers to deal with, and understand, these issues? How have teaching techniques evolved to accommodate these types of students? Imagine being handed the responsibility of teaching these varied classrooms. Imagine, in addition to multiple classified students in your room, you are also dealing with fidgety students and/or those who are suffering emotional issues due to technology.

As if this weren't complicated enough, there's another population of students affecting our schools and classrooms even more.

According to the Pew Research Center, prior to the COVID-19 pandemic, 14% of American children were living in poverty, that's just over 10 million American children living in homes with incomes below the federal poverty threshold[8]. That's a significant number of kids growing up in poor homes and/or communities—and it's safe to assume this number may have increased due to the recession caused by the Coronavirus outbreak.

When we hear the word "disparity," we tend to consider it solely in the context of economics. I see disparity as a term that can be applied in many ways. A child living in economic disparity suffers subsequent disparities as a result. They also experience nutritional, developmental, physiological, emotional, and educational disparities. They may also experience a disparity of the community, and, finally, disparity of the self.

---

8 Household income below $25,520 for a family of three.

A child growing up in a poor home does not have access to good and/or healthy food. This creates the nutritional and physiological disparities. Poor households typically exist in a world of constant stress, and this takes its toll developmentally and emotionally. If a child is growing up in a poor and/or dysfunctional community, he lacks a connection to that place. All of these affect the way a child learns—or doesn't—and so we see the educational disparity. Finally, all of these combined lead to a complete disparity of the self.

I speak of these disparities because I've seen them. I have taught in classrooms where a majority of my students were living in poverty, and I have seen what it does to young children as well as teenagers and adults. Poverty is horrific, and not just financially.

I've taught high school students who, immediately after school, take the bus back to their community, get off—only to jump on a public transit bus and go to work. They did not stop at home first. They would work from 4:00 p.m. until 10 or 10:30 at night. Finally, after another bus ride, they would arrive home close to midnight. These students had been awake since before 7:00 a.m., when the school bus picked them up. Homework? When could they possibly do it? And, mind you, these young people were not working because they wanted to or to make extra money. Their families needed them to work. In fact, they relied on it.

I have looked into the faces of six-year-olds and all the way to twenty-year-old students who were living in poverty. I have seen what this does to children, and it's terrible. In fact, it's tragic.

There is now insightful research and data telling us exactly what poverty does to children. It affects not only their neurological development but also cognitive development, as well as behavioral and emotional development—and we have over *10 million* children living in poverty nationwide. How do you think this—in addition to the aforementioned populations of kids—are affecting our public schools?

Children living in poverty are typically living with elements of stress that those of us not in poverty haven't considered. When schools closed en masse back in March and April 2020, due to COVID-19, many Americans were shocked to discover just how many American children lost access to their free breakfast and/or lunch.

Children living in poverty worry about the overall state of their siblings, and they also worry about their parents. Combined with this is the fact that many poor neighborhoods suffer excessive substance abuse, resulting in more stress.

I have taught special-needs students who—in addition—were living in poverty, and I watched helplessly as they became homeless. *I* was stressed out over this, so I can't imagine what they and their families were going through.

Scientific studies have shown that the brains of children living in poverty produce less gray matter. This is essential to brain functionality because it helps in the processing of memory, problem-solving, and language processing. Gray matter also affects behavioral issues such as impulse control and decision-making.

Again, I have experienced poor children coming into school and have watched them spend the first few hours of their day, literally, decompressing. By the time they finally settle down, they have to begin ramping themselves back up for the walk or bus ride home. It's a constant state of compress/decompress that I can't imagine living with. Of course, this is going to impact not only what and how they learn but also how they grow and develop a sense of who they are.

Children living in poverty are not playing outside, either, and this is primarily because they can't. I worked at an inner-city public school in Newark, New Jersey, and many of my students went home after school and did not leave their house until the next morning—when they came back to school. I had students as young as six and seven who I would walk home because their parents worked multiple jobs. Some students had witnessed violent crimes or were affected by crime through the death of a close friend or family member. This all impacted how they learned and behaved when they came into school.

Please understand that my point in relaying all of this information is not to portray a grim picture. My goal, rather, is to show the incredibly diverse reality of our public-school populations—and I don't just mean ethnically or culturally. I mean developmentally and socially.

Our children are not one singular thing. In fact, they are many things existing simultaneously, and that has always been the challenge of teaching. Trying to pull a classroom of many together to learn as one is difficult. This is now even more so, due to the developmental diversity of our students.

One of my teaching heroes is the late coach of the University of California Los Angeles (UCLA) men's basketball team, John Wooden. In the late 1960s and into the '70s, he won an unprecedented ten national championships—including an unbelievable run of seven in a row from 1967 to 1973. He also coached a number of future NBA greats and Hall of Fame players.

Wooden never viewed himself solely as a coach, but primarily as a teacher[9]. One of the things he believed was that a teacher cannot teach every student the same. This may seem obvious, but imagine how that applies to a teacher today. Imagine walking into a classroom and staring out into the wonderful faces of not just typically developing children but also some who are depressed. One is a high-functioning Autistic child; another has a slight learning disability. Maybe one is struggling with poverty; another's parents are getting divorced. This is the modern-day American public-school classroom. It is dynamic as well as developmentally and emotionally diverse, and it demands

---

9 In fact, Wooden believed that being a parent, teacher, and coach were all the same job. I agree 100%.

equally dynamic and creative teachers. This is how John Wooden coached his teams.

Wooden would begin each season by having every player on the team—regardless of year, position, or even if they were an All-American—come into the gym and engage in the same ritual: putting on their socks and sneakers. It was the simplest, yet most essential, act of playing basketball. If your socks and sneakers were not on the correct way—how were you going to do anything else right? The best part of this Wooden exercise was that he made the whole team sit and do it together. All-American seniors sat with brand-new freshmen. Non-starters were next to starters. It sent a message to the team right away: We're all on the same team, and we all begin every practice, game, and season the same way.

This is the biggest challenge facing American public schools: Bringing a classroom of diverse students together and getting them to work as one. How are teachers supposed to teach these diverse students today? How are we training our teachers to comprehend and effectively get through to multiple learning types at the same time? Are we training them in creative and dynamic techniques or methods?

I believe we need to update our teacher training. Part of this is creating awareness about the dynamics of the students now coming to school. The job of teaching is now more complex—and I don't mean this in a bad way. I mean it as someone who has been in a room of seven students who represented five different learning classifications. I say this out of affection for teaching varied populations of kids—and this is not exclusive to me; it's the experience of every public-school teacher in America today.

But what if there *were* something capable of reaching multiple populations of students at the same time? What if there were something that affected all students not just socially but also emotionally, neurologically, aesthetically, and physically? What if this singular thing could help students reset themselves emotionally, inspire physical movement, and encourage social and emotional expression?

It turns out there is, and it's been a part of our public school system almost since it began. I believe it can help move the whole of American public schools into its next phase—and do so at almost no significant cost.

That something is music.

3

MUSIC AND EDUCATION

Why Music?/It Goes Beyond Making You Better at Math/
Music and the Brain/Art and Education

When you woke up this morning, did you listen to music? Maybe you had a song running through your head, or maybe you had a radio station on. Maybe you have a smart speaker and called up some Mozart.

Perhaps you got into your car and listened to a specific playlist on the way to work and then to another on the drive home. Maybe you don't listen to music at all but ride in silence. Even if this is the case, at some point, you may hum a bar or two of your favorite song—or songs.

Maybe you stopped for coffee on your way. When you walked into the shop, there was undoubtedly music playing on the PA system. The car that pulled up next to you in the parking lot maybe had music blasting from the windows.

If you have children, think about how music is such a huge part of their lives. If they're still young, you probably have a song, or two, that you sing to them all the time. Maybe it's "Twinkle, Twinkle, Little Star" or "Livin' on a Prayer" by Bon Jovi.

While music is often thought of in the context of enjoyment or entertainment, think back to your childhood, and consider all of what you learned through songs or music. I grew up in the 1970s, and, on Saturday mornings, we watched animated programs for kids like *Scooby Doo*. A huge part of that ritual was little cartoon vignettes in between programs called *Schoolhouse Rock*.

These were two-to-three-minute shorts that used music to explain various elements of American life. If you don't know what I'm talking about or haven't seen them, most are available on YouTube. Just enter *Schoolhouse Rock*, and a menu of videos will appear, covering everything from grammar (adjectives, nouns, adverbs, and conjunctions), history (women's suffrage, the Revolutionary War), science (planets and electricity), math (multiplying by 3, multiplying by 4, the number 0), civic lessons (how a bill becomes a law), and even understanding how the human body works.

These seemingly silly little cartoons helped me—and my fellow '70s peers—better understand what we were learning in school. The best part is that we didn't realize how these cartoons were actually miniature lesson plans. To this day, as a 54-year-old married man with two children, my brain still jumps to the "Three Is a Magic Number" song from *Schoolhouse Rock* as well as "Conjunction Junction." The songs in these cartoons helped explain things through music and lyrics. We were unknowingly gaining a better understanding of school subjects—we just didn't realize it—and that's the magic of music.

I wrote earlier of technological advances and how they have affected scientific, medical, and academic research. A subsequent area significantly impacted by this research has been music, specifically related to how we process it and its overall effect on us.

This research, as well as my experience, allowed me to develop the primary thesis for this book, which is to further ask: What is the role that music should play in education? My question is not unique; it has intrigued humans from the beginning of time. Aristotle had thoughts on the subject, and, in *Politics*, he wrote:

*"It is not easy to determine the nature of music, or
why anyone should have a knowledge of it."*

After a lengthy dialogue, he concludes:

*". . . music has a power of forming the character and should,
therefore, be introduced into the education of the young."*

Echoes of Aristotle could be heard centuries later, when Charles Darwin wrote:

*"As neither the enjoyment nor the capacity of producing
musical notes is a faculty of the least benefit to man in
reference to his ordinary habits in life, they must be ranked
amongst the most mysterious with which he is endowed."*

Yes, music has always been perceived as possessing "strange powers"—and (as exemplified by Darwin) musical skills seem to be questioned as to what value they serve. But, as Aristotle noted, music has always played a role in our development. In some cultures, it has been used in a medicinal capacity. In others, it plays a spiritual role. Music provides not only entertainment but social outlets as well as emotional release. I believe that we take music for granted and that, in terms of its role in education, it is severely underused.

As stated earlier, our schools are now more developmentally, socially, and economically diverse than they've ever been. Our varied populations of students have caused a massive shift in all aspects of public education. Public schools now have to employ therapists, child-study teams, and classroom aides/paraprofessionals. We are at constant odds as to how we accommodate these varied learners in our schools. And while we come to terms with the fact that our schools must now provide services for these varied populations, we seem to be ignoring evidence that there is a singular thing out there capable of reaching multiple populations of students at the same time.

The amazing thing is that music has been a part of our public education system for decades and, yet, continues to be one of the first things trimmed, or cut, from a district's budget.

Over the course of time, we've also chosen to define "music education" through the highly restrictive definitions of either *band*, *chorus*, *orchestra*, or *general music*.

After centuries of writing about the "strange powers" we've always known music to possess, we are now—through the same scientific and technological revelations that helped with special education—gaining a more-comprehensive understanding of exactly what those "powers" are.

While ideas such as "Music calms the savage beast," and "It makes you better at math" have permeated our culture, scientific advances over the last twenty years have finally begun telling us exactly how music affects us. It has shown that music reaches us in ways no one could ever imagine.

A 2011 Finnish study found aspects of music like tone, timbre, and rhythm are separated within the brain and then stimulate different sections of the brain—including those responsible for emotions, creativity, and motor functions[10].

A study done in the Netherlands found that the simple act of listening to music affects your visual perception of the world around you[11]. In essence, taking a walk in the woods and listening to George Winston would give you a very different perception of the trees, leaves, light, and forms than if you were listening to Bad Brains.

Stanford School of Medicine produced research in 2007 that showed when short classical symphonies were played for subjects, "peak brain activity" occurred between movements—when there was no sound. The study went on to say:

". . . one possible adaptive evolutionary purpose of music is that it sharpens [the brain's] ability to anticipate events and sustain attention."[12]

---

10 *Science Daily*, December 6, 2011 https://www.sciencedaily.com/releases/2011/12/111205081731.htm

11 Ibid.

12 "Neural Dynamics of Event Segmentation in Music: Converging Evidence for Dissociable Ventral and Dorsal Networks" by Devarajan Sridharan, 1, 2,* Daniel J. Levitin, 4 Chris H. Chafe, 5 Jonathan Berger, 5 and Vinod Menon. Published in the August 2007 issue of *Neuron*

This study seems especially relevant when you consider the CDC report stating the rate of ADHD diagnosis among American kids is currently 9.8%. Perhaps the integration of these types of listening exercises—coupled with physical movement—would provide these classified students with a way to not only lengthen their attention spans, and increase focus, but to help organize themselves throughout the day.

How music affects our brains—and us—is something that is of interest to me, not just as a music educator but as a musician as well. Through my own personal experience of playing music and learning multiple instruments, I believe I can function and communicate better with large groups of people.

I also know that, because of my performance experience, I have no problems getting up in front of people to talk. My interest and studies in Latin music have led me to understand aspects of many Latin cultures I wouldn't have otherwise. I also believe that my studies in piano have made me more observant. When I was younger and hanging out in Manhattan punk-rock club CBGB[13], I watched many different artists and bands play live. Many of them made me realize that trying new things and stepping outside the mainstream could be pretty cool. Finally, the biggest thing music has taught me is the ability to sit alone and try new things while overcoming hours and hours and thousands upon thousands of mistakes. It has helped to make me very patient.

While these are my personal experiences, more and more scientific evidence continues to emerge that shows how music goes above and beyond in the way it affects us, and not just neurologically. We're now beginning to understand that it also affects us physically, emotionally, and socially.

Dr. Daniel J. Levitin is not just any neurologist. He's a neurologist who is also a musician—and not just any musician. Dr. Levitin is an accomplished professional musician and producer. He plays saxophone

---

13 I played in a band that was managed by the late owner of CBGB, Hilly Kristal.

and has worked with a wide array of artists, including the Grateful Dead, Joe Satriani, Santana, and many others. He holds a B.A. in Cognitive Psychology and Cognitive Science; he also holds a Ph.D. in Psychology. He also wrote the brilliant book *This Is Your Brain on Music.*

This first time I read *This Is Your Brain . . .* , I didn't know what to do. It literally stopped me in my tracks. I was, at the time, in the midst of studying Dalcroze Eurhythmics, and I was also doing an enormous amount of work with children on the Autism spectrum as well as children with cerebral palsy. I was lucky enough to be working closely with a wonderful group of occupational and physical therapists, while also working with my Eurhythmics teachers. It was a wonderful and enlightening time for me as a musician and educator.

Dr. Levitin's book could not have come at a better moment. I was witnessing children with special needs do things in my classes that they could not—or would not—do with their therapists. This wasn't just exciting, but puzzling. Why was this?

Our brains are extraordinarily complex. We are just beginning to scratch the surface when it comes to the understanding of them. Through my work with occupational therapists, one of the things I learned about was neuroplasticity—the brain's ability to reshape itself and form new neurological connections. Our brains can make adjustments throughout life that are based on experiences, environments, and even injuries. I never understood this idea until I got to work with children who have cerebral palsy.

Cerebral palsy (CP) is typically the result of a stroke suffered *in utero*. Because of this, the individual may lose the use of a hand, arm, leg, or, in extreme cases, an entire side of their body. They may also suffer a speech impediment. I worked with therapists who were treating children suffering through what is known as a *hemiplegia* of one hand or arm. This means they could not use one of their hands effectively. Their right hand might have functioned perfectly normally, but their left was incapable of complete and/or everyday function. The children were with the therapists to receive "constraint therapy."

When I first heard of constraint therapy it sounded somewhat mean. The children would come in and get their functional hand/arm fitted for a plaster cast—similar to what they'd get if they'd suffered a fracture. Once fitted, they would return a few days later to begin therapy. Their functional arm would be placed in the cast, and the children were made to go through typical activities such as eating, getting dressed, or brushing their teeth with their hemiplegic hand.

Upon initial witness, I felt terrible for the kids. On the first day in their casts, there was lots of struggle and frustration. Initially I didn't understand how the therapy worked, so I began talking to the therapists. In fact, I talked to them *a lot*. They told me about neuroplasticity and how it works. The whole purpose of the cast was to re-teach the brain how to signal the hemiplegic hand. Through a daily dose of regulated use (what the therapists called "blocked practice"), the brain would undergo various stages of plasticity—it would reconfigure itself to allow eventual functionality to the damaged hand. In other words, the brain "moved" different responsibilities to new areas or regions of the brain.

I remember the first day of therapy, watching the children eat lunch. There would be food all over the floor as well as the children themselves. By the end of three or four weeks, the lunchtime mess had decreased dramatically. Many of the children were able to pick up sandwiches and/or forks who hadn't been able to do so on the first day. It was amazing to observe.

As part of their therapy, the kids would come to me to participate in Eurhythmics-based musical exercises, also using their hemiplegic hands. I would do things like play the piano and have them hold thick sticks and drum along with my rhythm. As their therapy progressed, the sticks would grow thinner, causing them to use a tighter grip. I would also have them stand and move rhythmically to my piano music to help with their sense of balance and overall body awareness. The combination of working with the children and my Eurhythmics studies allowed me to come up with more ideas and games that enabled the kids to use their arms and bodies in different ways along with the music.

There were kids who wouldn't—or couldn't—do any of the "clinical"-type therapy activities, but they'd come to music and would do everything. The therapists would often use my session as a benchmark, just because they could see kids do things in music that they didn't see anywhere else. As my work with the kids and therapists went on, I continued to become more fascinated not just with neuroplasticity but also with how music affected the brain.

Dr. Levitin's book helped with this. I devoured it, and then I went back and read it again—and again. Many of the things he spoke about in his book were things that I was talking to the therapists about.

Through my Eurhythmics studies, I was taking movement classes and learning more about the body and how it worked. It was exciting to see how the subjects and activities matched up. One of the things Levitin wrote about in his book referenced how music affected multiple areas of the brain—not just one in particular. Basically, different regions of the brain process different elements of music, at the same time. Levitin writes:

"Musical activity involves nearly every region of the brain
that we know about, and nearly every neural subsystem."[14]

---

14 Levitin, pp 83 and 84

This falls in line with what the aforementioned Finnish study demonstrated. I witnessed aspects of this when working with the kids and therapists. What I saw were kids who did not respond to "rote"-based therapy (blocked practice). However, when a similar type of exercise (like moving a stick rhythmically) incorporated music, the kids were able to do it—and laughed while doing so. Was this because the sounds were stimulating sections of the brain not stimulated when music wasn't used?

A little girl who could not and would not pick up a fork, *would* pick up a stick and drum along with my piano playing. Not only that, she'd do it with an adorable grin.

The work I did with those children throughout those years made me very curious about the human brain. How does the brain work? I'll let Dr. Levitin provide a brief and very understandable explanation:

"The human brain is divided into four lobes—the frontal, temporal, parietal, and occipital—plus the cerebellum . . . The frontal lobe is associated with planning, self-control, and with making sense out of the dense and jumbled signals that our senses receive. The temporal lobe is associated with hearing and memory. The parietal lobe is associated with motor movements and spatial skills, and the occipital lobe with vision. The cerebellum is involved in emotions and planning of movements, and it is the evolutionarily oldest part of the brain."[15]

15 Levitin, p 83

When I read the above (and also dug deeper into the varied functionalities of the brain), my first question dealt with the cerebellum. Since this section of the brain is the oldest and is involved with both motor planning and emotions, does this link movement with emotion? When I read this, I immediately went back to the little girl who wouldn't pick up a fork but *did* pick up a stick and happily drummed along with my piano playing. Did the music help her connect those two things?

The playing of any musical instrument involves physical movement. In addition, one of the byproducts of listening to music is also . . . physical movement. This has always been the case. The ancient Greeks used music to get their armies to learn how to move and flow together. That is still the case with our modern-day troops. Rhythmic cadences like "Hut, two, three, four!" are staples on military bases around the world. A famous dictum by Socrates even states "The best dancer is also the best warrior".

Anthropologists agree that dance evolved out of music, and many believe that physical and emotional gesturing is a byproduct of dance. From its most primitive forms, music has always seemed to require a physical response of some kind. Whether it's a tapping of the foot or a full-blown Foxtrot, we all feel the urge to move to music.

Does this movement have an emotional purpose as well? Music is not just plain old notes but requires the musicians to shape those notes with their own emotions. The shape and dynamics that the musicians provide are what elicit our movements. It's amazing how musicians can essentially make their instruments "speak" emotions to us. Some even refer to this ability as "musical gesture." The composer Wagner once said that orchestras possess ". . . the faculty of uttering the unspeakable." He also believed that musical gesture and physical dance were the same thing.

The people of the African nation Lesotho (known as the Sesotho) have an expression, *Ho Bina*, which they use to describe both music and dance. They and many other cultures see the two as a singular thing. Physical movement and music are essential pieces of many cultures. I think it's time that we begin to see them as an essential piece to education.

As academic and scientific research has improved over the years, we have seen the incorporation of more and more movement-based therapies—and not just for individuals with physical disabilities. These therapies are now used also for those with developmental and emotional disabilities. This is not new; it is an extension of ideas that have existed for years.

Samuel Gridley Howe is a name that not many people are familiar with. Howe was a very progressive and valuable figure in the evolution of special education in the United States. Howe was born and raised in Boston, eventually earning a medical degree from Harvard in 1824. He then worked as a surgeon in Greece for five years. While there, he actually treated many patients who had been affected by Greece's war with Turkey.

Perhaps Howe was inspired by treating, helping, and then watching soldiers and citizens overcome their physical injuries. In any case, when he returned home, he established a school for the blind. In addition to publishing articles about physical injury, he also wrote about various treatments and theories on how the disabled could— and should—be educated.

Howe did not believe in looking down on the disabled. He did believe that, if treated correctly, individuals could overcome injuries and/or disabilities. Based on this belief, Howe developed raised-print books to accommodate the blind and help them read. This actually pre-dated the system that was created by Louis Braille.

Howe believed the disabled could ultimately be educated in public schools. He wrote extensively on this and lobbied hard for public-school reform. In 1848, he took his ideas and opened his own school for students who suffered mild physical and developmental disabilities.

A lot of what Howe provided in his school[16] in terms of therapy and practice was based on what he read, knew, and observed of the French physician Jean Marc Gaspard. Gaspard had worked extensively in treating children with physical and developmental disabilities and in 1807 wrote a highly regarded book on his successful treatment of an 11-year-old deaf boy: *The Wild Boy of Aveyron*.

Edouard Seguin, a student of Gaspard's, eventually developed his own methods for treating disabled individuals. His methods were primarily rooted in physical movement as well as sensory-based activities. Seguin believed that many of the delays his patients suffered were rooted in a "disconnect" between the mind and the senses. His education methods, which stressed physical and sensory-based exercises, inspired not only Howe but would also go on to inspire an Italian pediatrician named Maria Montessori. She would go on to found Montessori Schools, which are rooted in sensory-based learning and activities.

In one early photograph taken at Howe's school in 1903, there's a line of students in a gym, standing with arms on each other's shoulders. On one side is a woman, probably an aide or team teacher, with a piece of string attached to one boy's foot. She looks like she is possibly helping him establish a walking gait. At the head of the line is a male teacher facing the boys as they walk toward him. He has a drum strapped to his shoulder, and his sticks are tapping out a beat or cadence for the boys to move along with.

The idea of using musical rhythm to help humans with natural body movements is not a new idea. As stated earlier, the ancient Greeks used rhythm and movement to train their soldiers.

With advances in science, medicine, and technology, we are now beginning to understand why music inspires these movements. We're also beginning to discover that it goes even further than initially thought.

---

16 Which had the unfortunate name of "Massachusetts School for the Idiotic and Feeble-Minded"

New research now tells us that listening to music involves almost every region of the brain. When we hear a song or piece of music, it enters our brain through our ears and is then processed in the brain's stem. Our physical timing circuits are located in the stem of the brain, which may be why we begin physically tapping along. If you don't tap along physically, you may still do so mentally. If that's the case, these circuits would still "light up."

I recently attended a lecture on the use of music to treat people with Parkinson's disease. Videos were shown of individuals in whom the disease had advanced; it was hindering their walking gait as well as balance. One clip showed a man who was asked to walk across his living room. Because of tremors and a loss of body control, the task proved to be very difficult. But then, his favorite song was cued up (something by a Motown artist), and suddenly the man was able not only to walk across the room but also smile and dance. The tremors disappeared, and loss of balance disappeared.

The music therapist and author Dr. Dorita S. Berger, Ph.D., has written extensively on Eurhythmics-based applications, specifically in her work with children on the Autism spectrum. She defines music and how it's processed in the brain in the context of not just an art form but as energy. Music is, after all, energy traveling through time and space. Dr. Berger takes it a step further:

"... music, first, is acoustic energy. Energy is kinetic. Energy vibrates. When activated, energy moves across space from one source to another."[17]

17 Berger, pp 96 and 97

The vibrations are what causes the sounds. These musical sounds are more or less "decoded" in the brain stem (specifically in the *cochlear nuclei*) and are then passed into sections on both sides of the brain called the *auditory cortices*. Other sensory functions, such as smell, are also processed within the brain stem. As our brains are figuring the music out—or following along—subsequent sections get involved. It's also important to note that all of these sections are responsible for other activities as well. As an example, one section of our brain that gets involved with the decoding of the music is called the *hippocampus*. This section is also our memory center. Perhaps that's why a song or piece of music can inspire memories from years past and/or special events associated with them[18].

As the sounds and rhythms are further processed, sections of the brain known as the *cerebellar vermis* and *amygdala* also get involved. These are where a vast majority of our emotional processing occurs. The frontal lobes, which control motor planning, and the sensory cortex are also lighting up.

The fact is, music is a full-on neurological event—in addition to being a physical *and* emotional event. The emotional aspect of music is vital. I believe this is why we humans choose to mark so many of the emotional points in our lives (birthdays, holidays, weddings, proms, funerals) with music. We associate many of our emotional moments with songs.

Incredibly, our brain will incorporate other sections, depending on if we're listening to music, playing an instrument, or even conducting. This is also the case if we're just reading music or lyrics and/or singing along.

I always tell my students that, when they're playing an instrument or singing along, they're using their entire bodies. Often, they look

---

18 To this day, when I hear "Open Arms," by Journey, I hear and smell my high school cafeteria.

at me like I'm crazy or—in the case of high school kids—just *tell* me I'm crazy. That's when I write this on the board:

Music:

- **Hear It:** Melody, harmony, lyrics, sounds, rhythms
- **See It:** Notes, lyrics
- **Speak It:** Lyrics, "Oohs" and "Aahs"
- **Move It:** Playing your instrument, clapping, stomping, dancing, swaying, breathing, singing
- **Feel It:** Emotions

As I write it, I typically hear a murmur of acknowledgment in the room. Many have never realized what is happening when they play, listen to, or sing music. Many have told me that, after I write this list down, they look at their musical experiences quite differently.

As questions regarding modern education and learning are at the forefront of national discussion, we need to acknowledge the fact that our public schools are more developmentally and economically diverse. When the topics of education reform and/or education policy come up, you never hear anyone speak of our special-needs students. My question is: Why not? How could these populations—7 million of them—not be discussed outwardly when reform topics are broached? How could the fact that these children, and their needs, who have reshaped the public-education landscape *not* be a significant piece of any education-reform conversation?

Many public-school districts are scrambling to accommodate these populations. Remember, a significant number of school districts in the nation have been impacted by this, and I don't mean this in a disparaging way. I mean it as fact. I'm going to say it again: Public school districts across the country are trying to find necessary ways and methods to accommodate these students.

The best way is already a part of our education system and has been for decades.

Thanks to advances in technology, science, and medicine, we now have evidence showing us how much of our brains are, in fact, stimulated by music. It would appear music enhances our understanding of everything—including ourselves.

As I stated earlier, I believe education to be a journey of self-discovery. It is not solely a process that involves stuffing facts and figures into the heads of children. I tend to view the job of teachers more as guiding students to understand how things work. Once that understanding is complete, teachers then use methods and ways to show students how they can apply them to real-world functioning as well as new ideas of their own.

Modern-day education, with its heavy emphasis on testing, flies in the face of the facts I wrote about earlier. The kids coming to school today are much more socially, emotionally, economically, and developmentally diverse. Many come to school not aware of who they are or who they want to be. While this is normal, the current cultural and social climate, with its emphasis on social media, affects this process. Many also have a classification (diagnosis) or are coming to school out of poverty. This complicates the process of self-discovery that is education.

Adding to this is what I call the "Professionalization of Childhood"—suddenly, kids aren't allowed to be kids anymore. Beginning as young as six and seven years, children are being told they have to pick their sport, begin working toward scholarships, and/or preparing for college. Every aspect of their lives—both academic and recreational—now has a purpose and/or reason. It's no longer for discovery or enjoyment.

I recently had a student's parent say to me, "She's just not passionate about anything." My immediate thought was *She's seven! She needs to just be enjoying and discovering things!* I saw and heard similar things at my own children's sporting events as they were growing up. Age or ability did not matter. Beginning at age five, the word "scholarship" was bantered about constantly. Kids who two or three years ago needed a nap to get through the day were suddenly expected to understand hitting a baseball as well as, if not better than, Ted Williams.

Another addition making education more complex is the online grade book. Students (and their parents) now have twenty-four-hour access to every grade for every class. The second a grade is posted or entered, students (and parents) receive an email update where they can click and check the portal. I recently had a high school piano student come in for her lesson one day looking utterly upset and dejected. "What's wrong?" I asked.

"A math grade was posted in the middle of the day, and my mom called and yelled at me. I hadn't even seen it. Then my dad texted me, and he was mad, too."

The grade causing all of this uproar: 87 (out of 100).

With all of this pressure, how are kids supposed to learn and discover who they are? How are they to become themselves?

The great jazz pianist Thelonious Monk said:

"The genius is the one who's most like himself."

This is such a beautiful statement for many reasons. If you think about the women and men throughout history who are hailed as geniuses, they are so because they were true to themselves. To the rest of us, they seem "unique" or perhaps "quirky," and that's because they *are that*—and guess what? So are *all of us*. We are all different! We all hold unique perspectives. Have you ever watched a group of young children dance? It's amazing. The reason it's so amazing is because, while they're all hearing the same song and feeling its beat, they all move differently. They're all smiling, and they are *all* being themselves.

I have two children, and they could not be any more different. Yes, they are also alike in many ways, but in terms of how they think and socialize—and regarding their general interests—they are completely different. This is the case with all of us, and is especially the case with how we grow, develop, and learn. It is the job of teachers to make sure that students understand their individual and unique perspective, and enable them not only to learn but also to become themselves—and, due to our more-diverse student populations, this responsibility has now become more complex.

Music can help all teachers with this.

The emerging research regarding music and the brain is also helping us to understand how music affects our emotional and social development. There is a new field of study emerging called *neuroaesthetics*, geared toward researching how the arts affect our perception and understanding of the world and those around us. Neuroaesthetic research has begun delving into how the arts affect not only our brain but also our emotions.

We have all attended some kind of arts performance, whether it's a gallery opening, movie, dance recital, symphony orchestra, opera, or a rock concert. Consider that, when you attend one of these, you rarely do so alone. If you do go alone, once you arrive, there are other people there—and you're all there for the same reason: to experience something.

Think about what happens when you walk into the space: How you feel, what you look at, what you listen for. If it's a gallery or museum, you're typically standing in a room with others, admiring paintings and/or sculptures. Maybe you share observations with those around you. These could be verbal, simple nods, or facial expressions. You may comment about the use of color, light, and imagery. This seemingly "still" gallery has suddenly become a social space—and what are you discussing? How the art pieces are moving you. You're feeling and expressing the emotions running through you and sharing them with others—and you all see and feel something different.

The same happens at live-concert events. You are standing (or sitting) in a hall or arena full of mostly strangers. The lights go down, the music starts, and suddenly you're dancing and moving together. You're waving your arms in the air. You're smiling. I was once at a Bob Dylan concert, and not only did he sound great that particular night, but his song selection was unbelievable. I was standing by myself but turned to a husband and wife next to me. Based on seeing their facial expressions (and them seeing mine), we were all bursting with excitement at what was happening on stage. We didn't have to introduce ourselves or shake hands. Suddenly a husband, wife, and complete stranger were verbally sharing an emotional moment that was also social.

This was in response to music

Now consider how much we all missed these things during the COVID lockdowns. Not having concerts, museums, dance clubs, and ballet performances has had an extraordinary impact on our overall mental health, and added to our sense of isolation.

When we're at a social event such as a concert, sections of our brain are being stimulated just from being among a crowd. Humans are social animals. We enjoy interacting with others, and our brains are attuned to things like the facial expressions and body movements of people around us. The sections of the brain known as the *medial prefrontal cortex* and the *temporoparietal junction* are stimulated.

It's no coincidence that rhythm and pitch are two musical elements that stimulate the prefrontal cortex. This section of the brain is also where decision-making, behavior, and expression are controlled. All of this neuroactivity is not exclusive to a single individual at a concert. It's happening to everyone.

Our brains also possess what's called a *mirror neuron system*. These neurons react to the movements of people around us and literally begin to fire in response to other's physical movements. We may physically respond and begin imitating those movements. Think of the concert: the music starts, and the person in front of you stands up and begins to dance. You may watch for a second, but then the people to your right and left stand up. Before you know it—everyone is up. The movements and sounds are a full-on sensory experience. Your brain is being stimulated not only by the music but also by the people around you. Our mirror neuron systems allow us to respond to those around us and then share with everyone. If those around you are moving in a way that makes you laugh or smile, you imitate those movements, thus sharing those emotions. This process spreads throughout the whole arena.

We key off of each other's movements—and not just physically. We also respond to them emotionally and socially. Think of hugs and handshakes (pre-COVID-19). When someone extends their hand, it's not only a gesture, but one of goodwill and friendly feelings. If it's among business people, then it's a bond or show of trust. A hug is a sign of love and comfort. Children hug their parents; husbands hug wives. Longtime male friends bring it in for a "bro hug." The point is that our physical movements are also a form of communication. They elicit responses that are physical, emotional, and social.

This response even occurs neurologically. Say, for example, you're attending a much more subdued musical performance—the ballet, opera, or symphony. When at such events, standing and clapping or dancing during the performance is not a general practice. We tend to watch these performances from our seats. Even though we're sitting, our mirror neurons are stimulated through watching the movements—and, while we may not stand up, our mirror neurons still allow us to "move."

When we hear a symphony orchestra perform, we don't just listen to the music. We also witness the musicians moving, as well as the conductor. The violin section may be playing a staccato-like passage that requires quick arm movements. In contrast, the horns may be playing deeper and longer legato-type notes. We respond to those sounds as well. Our mirror neurons allow us to see and feel ourselves moving along with the music. The same goes for watching a ballet. A dancer is twirling on stage, and we can *feel* those movements inside our own body.

The human brain—and thus physiology—responds to art in emotional ways. We see the stories being told in an opera or a ballet and feel what the characters feel. We hear the music of an orchestra and feel what the music is "saying." It speaks directly to us—and not just through the notes being played. There are the physical movements of the musicians and the conductor, as well as the physical movement of the music: the ups and downs of the pitches as well as dynamics (volume), the rhythm, and the articulation of the beats (quick or long).

There are many scientists who believe that we actually take all of these aspects of performance and imprint them into our sensory systems. We walk away from a concert with an aesthetic sense of the experience. I believe it's important for me to note that the word "aesthetic" is rooted in the ancient Greek word *aisthesis*. The Greeks used this word to define the human ability to mentally bring together the experiences of the senses. Through scientific study, we are now beginning to realize that the Greeks were not far off. Through our

mirror neurons, we are taking in the sights and sounds of a performance, and they engulf our bodies, not just physically but also
emotionally and socially.

Imagine harnessing this power to help our children in school.
Imagine harnessing this power so that classroom teachers can better
understand the developmentally diverse students in front of them.
Imagine harnessing this power to help our kids better understand who
they are and who they can be. Imagine using this power to improve
the overall social and emotional climate of our kids.

4

HOW DALCROZE EURHYTHMICS CAN HELP TRANSFORM PUBLIC EDUCATION

Music Is Movement/Emile Jaques-Dalcroze/Eurhythmics as Music Education/Eurhythmics as a Teacher Training Tool

It is not uncommon to hear the term "music and movement." As a music educator, I hear it a lot. Typically, it's in the context of "I'm signing my child up for a movement-and-music class." I myself used to use the term quite frequently, and (full disclosure) the name of my program, TumbleJam™, actually uses the phrase in its name ("Music, Movement, Fun").

After completing a three-year study in Eurhythmics, I stopped using the terms separately from one another because I became aware of the fact that they're the same thing. Music is the byproduct of physical movement. Without it, we do not get sound, and we also do not get beat, phrasing, or dynamics. Our physical movements produce and shape the notes that come out of our instruments. And if we're not playing the instruments making the sounds, we're physically responding to the music that's being made by them.

I think this is very important to note regarding the evolution in modern education—especially when it comes to the role of music.

Many tend to look at music education solely through the lens of band, orchestra, chorus, and general music class. Perhaps they view it through two or more of those. I believe the modern lens of music education needs to expand and—in addition to the aforementioned—also include Eurhythmics classes. In fact, I believe that public schools should also have separate Eurhythmics teachers on staff, in addition to music teachers. They, like occupational, speech, and social-skills therapists, would be available to the student body. However, they would also be available to classrooms and their teachers. I also believe that all teachers (not just music) should go through a three-week course of Eurhythmics training.

Why?

In order to understand what Eurhythmics is, one must understand the man who created it, Émile Jaques-Dalcroze. I believe that he was way ahead of his time, and not just in how he developed his method. Dalcroze did not just consider how Eurhythmics would apply to the training of musicians but eventually saw it in the context of the whole of education. He was looking past music for music's sake. Who was Émile Jaques-Dalcroze, and why did he create this method of teaching?

Émile Henri Jaques was born in Vienna in 1865. His parents were both Swiss, and his mother, Julie, was a music teacher. Julie was well versed in the teaching methods, writings, and philosophies of Johann Heinrich Pestalozzi, who believed in teaching through the senses and self-experience.

Émile grew up around music and learned piano from his mother. When he was ten, his parents moved to Geneva, Switzerland, where, after high school, Émile enrolled at the Geneva Conservatory. He would eventually make his way to Paris, France, where he studied drama but also maintained his musical studies at the Paris Conservatory. It was in Paris where Émile discovered the writings and teachings of Mathis Lussy, a piano teacher who wrote extensively on the art of expressive performance.

One focus of Lussy's writings was on the role of breath in playing music. He did not see breathing as simply an act of living but a natural way of keeping time. In fact, Lussy almost defines breathing as a musical act itself, describing the inhale and exhale as a "dynamic curve." Lussy's attention to the physiological aspects of playing intrigued Émile and would make a lasting impression on him.

In 1886, Émile took a job conducting in Algiers, a French colony in northern Africa at the time. This is when he formally changed his name from "Émile Jaques" to "Émile Jaques-Dalcroze." This was because there was a French composer (primarily of polka music) with whom he did not want to be confused.

After a year in Algiers, Dalcroze returned to Vienna and began studying at the Conservatory. It is important to mention this because, while in Vienna, Dalcroze was exposed to a very strict teacher. This helped him to realize that an effective teacher does not simply yell to get results but approaches teaching with the whole child in mind.

In 1892, Dalcroze returned to Geneva and began teaching solfege (ear and voice training) at the Geneva Conservatory. This is when he first observed how many of his students were solid technically but lacked musicality. He also noticed that many of his students had a difficult time holding or keeping a steady beat. These things began to both worry and intrigue him. Dalcroze made a point of observing how his students had difficulties recognizing and feeling the "small nuances" in music. I think it's interesting that he chose to use the word "nuances" to define his students' problems. Mathis Lussy refers to "musical nuances" specifically when writing about things like musical expression, tempo, and accents.

Despite frustration with his students, Dalcroze did observe certain things that served as inspiration along the way. One of them was the subtle movements of feet or hands tapping while his students sang. They were never just singing.

Dalcroze began to consider these small, nuanced movements that his students demonstrated. As he was pondering them in his office one day, he looked out the window and saw a student walking across the conservatory campus. He observed the natural rhythms in their gait and stride—the way the body parts moved and flowed together. This inspired one of the earliest Eurhythmics-type exercises he would use in class.

In another experience, Dalcroze came off the train one day and encountered a student who had trouble feeling musical rhythms in music. As the two were making their way to class it began to rain. Both Dalcroze and his student began running in an effort to not get wet, but also because they were a bit late. As they picked up their pace and began to run, Dalcroze noticed the student was able to change his walking rhythm to running rather seamlessly. Dalcroze began to purposely alter his pace from fast to slow and back again, and the student was able to, again, change his rhythm and "follow" along. This "a-rhythmic" student actually possessed physical rhythm. This experience served Dalcroze as further inspiration.

These experiences served as inspiration for subtle changes in Dalcroze's teaching. In an effort to get his students to understand rhythm better, he simply had his students begin class by walking around the room. While they moved, he asked them to observe and feel the rhythm of their own walk. He also asked them to observe their classmates. This was not just a simple physical act. By having his students do this, they were adapting to the space physically and socially. They weren't just walking around the room and feeling the space but seeing and acknowledging the others around them—and embodying the physical movements of their peers.

As someone who has taught special-needs children, the most thrilling thing about learning this was how the basic idea for Dalcroze's method evolved from wanting students to first gain an idea of their own body—their own self. He, literally, had his students walk around the room and *feel* themselves in space. *Feel* themselves move. They were also able to *feel* and see the movements of their classmates.

The simple act of asking his students to walk served as inspiration. Dalcroze began adding musical elements to this exercise. He would improvise pieces on the piano and ask his students to walk in time with his playing. As things progressed, bigger movements like arm swings were added—all done in time while students were walking with the music.

He eventually asked his students to remove their shoes and socks when they came to class, in addition to wearing loose-fitting clothing. Both of these helped students move more freely and also feel their body positions better.

All of these inspirations and developments came about because Dalcroze witnessed what he called a "disconnect" between his students' minds and bodies.

It's important to remember how Dalcroze was teaching in a period of time that, historically and technologically speaking, is not unlike today. He was making his observations in the late nineteenth century. The Industrial Revolution had systematically changed the way people worked and lived. Factory life was how many Europeans were earning their living. Society itself had become mechanized, and many people had relocated to live in cities. In other words, there was a massive societal shift, and significant aspects of the way people lived had drastically changed. Dalcroze acknowledged this when he wrote about this time as one of "social reconstruction."

Dalcroze also felt the subjects being taught at his conservatory were ". . . too fragmentary and specialized." He also felt that his fellow music faculty were:

". . . confined to his own narrow domain, having practically no contact with those of his colleagues who specialize in other branches of musical science."[19]

Perhaps it's safe to say the holistic approach that Dalcroze was in the process of developing was at odds with what he saw around him. He was beginning to understand and see the connection between music and life.

When I read Dalcroze now, I can't help but think of how he would have responded to our public schools today. He used so much language that is applicable to what modern educators (and not just music) are experiencing. He wrote about the importance of educating children's "nervous faculties" as well as their "mental calm and concentration." He also wrote about the importance of making students aware of the relationship between their minds and ". . . the conscious and the subconscious, between imagination and the processes of action."

In his mind, Dalcroze believed that "Thoughts should be brought into immediate contact with behavior—the new education aiming at regulating interaction between our nervous and our intellectual forces."

Dalcroze viewed his students as whole beings. He didn't look at them solely as *music students*, but as human individuals who needed to learn about themselves before they could be taught anything else—and that included music. However, he also recognized that the dynamic qualities in music could help him accomplish this.

---

19 Dalcroze, p 6

He also defined learning as an act involving the senses. One of the senses he described as being vital is what he called "inner hearing." This concept played a big role in the evolution of his methods and many of the games that he devised to accompany them.

Another key component of Eurhythmics is what Dalcroze called "quick-reaction" games. One example would be a game where students move around the room rhythmically to music on the piano and either change direction or maybe change their step when a certain musical cue or interval is played. The game may ask that students stop when the music stops. Whatever the response, the teacher improvises a tune and begins by putting the cue or interval at the end of a musical phrase. The students hear the phrase two or three times and now assume they know when the next change/reaction is coming—the musical cadence. That's when the teacher switches it up and tricks them.

Quick-reaction games force students to listen not only with their ears but with their entire body—they're listening while moving around the room and anticipating a physical response. I have played these games in my classes, and when the initial trick comes, the response is always the same: the class cracks up laughing. It doesn't matter if it's a class of developmentally disabled kids, at-risk inner-city high school students, or a group of middle school music teachers: They all laugh. However, when the game resumes, they all focus a bit more. Now they know the "trick" is coming—they just don't know when or where in the music. As I play, I can see their expressions becoming more focused—but their movements become more fluid. It's almost as if they know they're now listening within themselves as well as with their body.

Dalcroze eventually named his method "Eurhythmics"—rooted in the Greek *eu* and *rhythmos*, which translates as "good flow." From the beginning, he recognized how music is movement. In 1909, he wrote, in an essay titled "Rhythm as a Factor in Education":

*"Before teaching the relation which exists between sound
and movement, it is wise to undertake the independent
study of each of these two elements. Movement is instinctive
in man and therefore primary. Therefore I begin the study
of music by careful experimental teaching of movement."*

He writes of the importance of Eurhythmics not only as a method
to teach music but also as a way to connect mind and body and give
the students an understanding of themselves:

*"The object of the method is, in the first instance, to
create by the help of rhythm a rapid and regular current
of communication between brain and body."*

Finally, he shows how this connection is important in developing
not only musical ability but the whole of self-expression:

*"The education of the nervous system must be of such a nature
that the suggested rhythms of a work of art induce in the
individual analogous vibrations, produce a powerful reaction
in him, and change naturally into rhythms of expression . . .
But I assert that the experiments in rhythm, and the complete
study of movements simple and combined ought to create a
fresh mentality, that artists thus trained will find inevitably
and spontaneously new rhythmic forms to express feelings,*

*and that in consequence their characters will be able to
develop more completely and with greater strength."*[20]

Consider those words in the context of the student populations I defined earlier. I believe it makes them more powerful—as well as relevant. Again, 14% of the American public school population is composed of students who need special-education services—more than 7 million children nationwide. Within that population, 34% have specific learning disabilities.

Eurhythmics could be a powerful tool in the teaching of these populations. It allows a holistic approach for the teacher and the student. It is a way for students to begin to feel and understand themselves as well as a way for the teacher to see and understand them.

As Dalcroze continued to hone his methods, he began to hear, and see, results from his students. Word began spreading among his fellow faculty members. Colleagues came to observe him, and, not surprisingly, some of his methods and techniques were deemed questionable. It was, after all, the late nineteenth century. Perhaps the "stuffy" conservatory faculty were unprepared as they entered Dalcroze's classroom and witnessed barefooted men and women in loose-fitting clothes moving freely around the room . . . in close proximity. Upon further scrutiny, Dalcroze was labelled a "radical." Some even referred to his exercises as "monkeyshines".

Despite the less-than-favorable views among his Geneva colleagues, Dalcroze's work began gaining a sense of positive interest. The administration in the conservatory may have been puzzled or put

20 Dalcroze/Harvey, p 21

off by Eurhythmics, but the citizens of Geneva saw its value. They not only encouraged Dalcroze's practice and teaching, but sent their children to his classes. This allowed Dalcroze to further develop his methods and philosophies, and eventually, word began to spread about Eurhythmics outside of Geneva.

Dalcroze was eventually invited to give a demonstration class in Berlin, Germany. This was greeted with such overwhelming positivity that he was invited to create a school in Hellerau, Germany, which is located just outside of Dresden. The invitation to Dalcroze came from a man named Wolf Dohrn, who was an economist interested in social development specifically through the use of the arts.

The significance of the school in Hellerau and the role it played in the evolution of Eurhythmics can be a separate book and/or research paper unto itself. The school was not a *school* in the sense that we think of. It was more like an artist colony/wellness spa. The city of Hellerau was a place where people went to relax. It was known as a "garden city," with wide-open space and access to nature. This was reflected in the architecture and aesthetic of the school. It spoke not only to what Dalcroze was trying to accomplish but also to the creative vision of a number of individuals.

The buildings and grounds were developed by German architect Heinrich Tessenow, whose ideas were inspired by the English Arts and Crafts movement—a movement that wanted to get back to individualized designs and move away from the "cookie cutter" aesthetic brought on by mass production of the industrial revolution.

Tessenow's buildings have a Greek look and feel but are not ornamental. The interiors are open, spacious, and available for self-expression. Tessenow designed the interior of the main building based on the ideas of stage designer Adolphe Appia and the vision of Dalcroze. This building was one of the first to have a retractable orchestra pit. Pieces of the stage could be moved around, as could the audience seats.

When the school was completed in 1911, its overall aesthetic was one of connection and awakening. The combination of Tessenow's designs and Appia and Dalcroze's ideas had created a progressive school of the arts. It represented a place where students of all ages could come and present as well as open themselves up.

This aesthetic is present in the writings of Ethal Ingham, a student from England, who attended Hellerau in 1911:

> *"Surely never before has the world held better opportunities*
> *for studying and loving the beautiful and true. One*
> *need be but a few days in Hellerau in order to see*
> *some of the many advantages a stay has to offer."*

She continues further regarding the design:

> *"The college itself is a fine example of the value of*
> *simplicity and space in architecture. Both without and*
> *within, the block of buildings is impressive, this effect*
> *being gained by an extreme simplicity of decoration."*[21]

I should note that Ingham's father, Charles, was himself an educator and had observed Eurhythmics classes in Geneva. He was so taken with what he saw that he took his family (Ethal amongst them) to Hellerau. Charles also published the first article about Eurhythmics

---

21 Dalcroze/Harvey, pp 44–46

in the English language, titled, "Music and Physical Grace, the New Rhythmic Gymnastics."

In addition to the design of the facilities, there were (of course) the classes offered to students. While the students were there to study with Dalcroze, they were also able to take lessons on individual instruments. Drawing lessons were also offered. The students were also encouraged to go into Dresden to see local performances. The classes, combined with the natural surroundings, helped to create a unique learning environment. As Ms. Ingham again observed:

"An atmosphere of enthusiasm and good-will permeates the social life. No community of the kind could have a more delightful spirit of unity than that which pervades the Jaques-Dalcroze School. All students are keen and anxious to live as full a life as possible; everyone will willingly and unselfishly take time and trouble to help others who know less than themselves."[22]

The school at Hellerau was, indeed, unique in its design and intention, but also because it represented the first place Dalcroze offered extended classes. It was the first place a student could go and study Eurhythmics exclusively.

---

22 Dalcroze/Harvey, p 45

Hellerau began to attract students primarily from all over Europe. Those who attended did not come in classified solely as "music" or "Eurhythmics" students. They were, rather, able to simultaneously call themselves dancers, actors, and musicians. This was reflected in the summer of 1912, when the school presented a public performance of Gluck's "Orpheus and Eurydice." They also presented a demonstration of Dalcroze's improvisation exercises and group rhythmic classes. Students appeared on stage and were not listed as musicians, dancers, or actors—but as all three.

In the summer of 1913, a second public performance of "Orpheus and Eurydice" was presented, this time to an audience of 5,000 people. In the audience were many great European thinkers as well as artists—playwright George Bernard Shaw among them. Many believe the work Dalcroze was doing at the school helped to spur a modernist movement throughout Europe.

Others who attended classes, or saw performances, included the German artist and thinker Henry van de Velde as well as Prince Sergai Wolkonsky from Russia—who was also the Superintendent of the Imperial Russian Theatre.

I think it's safe to say the school at Hellerau is where Eurhythmics classes took flight. Again, Dalcroze offered classes to students of all ages and professions, and he was offering them not only for the purpose of musical training. As Ms. Ingham wrote:

"One need be but a few days in Hellerau in order to see some of the many advantages which a stay has to offer. For men and women searching for a profession in life; for those fresh from school while waiting to discover their natural

bent; for adults who seek a change from their ordinary surroundings and who wish to improve in culture and in health; for musicians and students in art, for teachers of dancing, and for children of all ages, a course of study at the College in Hellerau contains advantages and opportunities which seem to exist in no other educational institution."[23]

Dalcroze's students were dynamic and diverse—like our public schools today. The courses offered were not viewed through one scope but were, rather, seen through many lenses. Students came to Hellerau and gained not only more of an artistic insight but also a more-developed sense of self. They were able to awaken from within. I think Ms. Ingham sums it up best:

"A change is often observable in pupils after they have been but a few weeks in residence, a change which tells of more alertness of mind, of more animated purpose, and even higher ideals and aims in life."[24]

From the start of his classes, Dalcroze's aim was not one thing. Yes, his methods are rooted in and inspired by music, but the overall

---

23 Dalcroze/Harvey, p 44
24 Dalcroze/Harvey, p 46

goal is not solely musical. His methods speak to a larger purpose as well as to a diverse room of individuals—not just musicians. What he wrote in "Rhythm as a Factor in Education" is a testament to this:

"The first result of a thorough rhythmic training is that the pupil sees clearly in himself what he really is and obtains from his powers all the advantage possible."

I believe Dalcroze saw the connection between self-awareness and mind/body as the most important skill in all of education—not just music education. He continues:

"All modern educationalists are agreed that the first step in a child's education should be to teach him to know himself, to accustom him to life, and to awaken in him sensations, feelings, and emotions . . ."

Early on in the Hellerau school's existence, there was a doctor's convention in Dresden. A group of pediatricians made a trip to

Hellerau specifically to observe Dalcroze's work. They also brought a new perspective: scientific. Upon observing classes and demonstrations the doctors were collectively impressed. One made specific note about how Eurhythmics attended to the nervous system. After a day of observation and questions, the group of pediatricians left Hellerau with a common verdict: Eurhythmics should be a part of the public school curriculum.

Dalcroze recognized music and all of its dynamic qualities as a way to develop and educate students for everything. His methods were the byproduct of a changed world—a society that, much like today, had experienced monumental shifts not just in work but in its culture. The industrial age had taken hold of society and had impacted every facet of life. As a result, education and the way students learned and developed was also being reexamined—again, much like today. The need for self-discovery was something Dalcroze recognized, and I think his methods speak to that—I also believe that in the wake of the COVID-19 pandemic and subsequent school closings, this aspect of education cannot be emphasized enough. Imagine the benefits Eurhythmics classes can provide when school's resume as "normal"?

The other important aspect of the way Dalcroze developed his method was his willingness to use Eurhythmics to teach all ages. In our modern day, specifically among music educators, Eurhythmics is generally seen as a method only for younger children. Rarely does one encounter an American middle or high school where Eurhythmics exercises or techniques are included in the music curriculum. The school at Hellerau was open to students of all ages: children to adults.

As I stated at the beginning of this book, I have used my Eurhythmics training with (literally) every type of student. This includes various ages and abilities. I have used Eurhythmics with at-risk inner-city high school students — some who were as old as nineteen and twenty. Their age didn't matter. I do not think this was/is an accident. I believe Dalcroze created Eurhythmics with all students and all ages in mind. Again, this is much more pertinent in the face of the COVID-19 pandemic.

Eurhythmics is a dynamic method and helps teachers become more holistic in their approach. It trains teachers to look at students as the dynamic individuals they are. We Dalcroze teachers view our students physically, emotionally, creatively, aesthetically, and, most of all, as humans.

Because of its dynamic approach, Eurhythmics helps teachers accomplish two things: First, it teaches teachers to understand themselves. A beginner Dalcroze teacher is taught to move and to be uninhibited. I remember, on my first day of Dalcroze training, being blown away as my teacher began improvising a sweeping piece on the piano. Without hesitation, my fellow barefooted classmates suddenly began freely moving around the room. I was left sitting alone in my chair momentarily in a state of shock while the others in the room immediately responded to the music.

The physical movement is but one piece of the training. We are taught solfege, but we are taught the Dalcroze way. Solfege training in college (or high school) is more often than not a boring affair, in which students are asked to recognize and sing musical intervals, typically sitting in chairs. These classes involve references to musical distances such as minor thirds and major fifths. A singular pitch is played on the piano and students are asked to sing a major second from it while the rest of the students sit and listen. There may be some group singing, but, by and large, students are seated, and the mood in the room is one of general drudgery and nervousness.

A Dalcroze solfege lesson exploits the interval distances not just in the context of musical pitches, but also through physical space, movement, and gesture. In a Dalcroze class, musical steps turn into physical steps. A major fifth is represented through five physical steps or perhaps a colorful illustration on the board. Maybe an interval is used to tell a story as students move around the room to improvised music. The boring drudgery of college solfege is turned into joy. It is no longer just notes. It becomes musical representation through physical movement. It becomes aesthetic.

The final piece of being a Dalcroze teacher is learning how to improvise—a necessity for a teacher to accompany a class of dynamic students accordingly. I personally loved this aspect, because, in addition to learning how to improvise on the piano, it taught me how to better accommodate an energetic class of students whose whims, ideas, and movements change on a dime. In other words, Eurhythmics training didn't just influence me musically, but also in my collective teaching.

Improvisation is more than a way to accompany movement; it's also a way to establish a healthy class dynamic. In modern terms: improvisation is a great classroom-management technique. I also believe my improvisational training helped me quickly adapt when the COVID-19 pandemic hit. I was able to make the sudden pivot from live to virtual classes, literally within a day of being told. I began uploading Dalcroze videos to a new YouTube channel and made them available to my students. Almost immediately I heard from thankful parents. I even received a video from the mother of a developmentally disabled daughter, which showed her moving along to one of my videos and smiling.

In the midst of the COVID-19 pandemic, I was contacted by a group of Dalcroze teachers who were organizing a community Zoom meeting. How to effectively use Dalcroze over video was openly discussed. One teacher based in Colorado shared a camera he had purchased that actually moved with him around his studio. Teachers shared ideas and experiences. The general consensus was that making the move to video didn't present too many challenges.

There were Dalcroze teachers from America as well as ones from all over the world. We began meeting on a tri-weekly basis—again for the purpose of discussing methods and ideas. At times, I felt that I wasn't speaking with a Zoom meeting full of teachers. I was, rather, speaking with artists.

Dalcroze training shows teachers how to learn wholly. You emerge from the training with a better understanding of yourself. I don't see Eurhythmics as a teaching technique but as a system—one that teaches teachers to learn through the body. If I may quote the choreographer Faustin Linyekula:

"Where I came from, no knowledge system is complete until it goes through the body."

The second thing Dalcroze training accomplishes is that it truly teaches teachers how to impart this knowledge to their students. In Dalcroze training, you are observing other teachers beginning, literally, the first day of training—and these are all levels of Dalcroze teachers. You are in a room watching certified and/or licensed Dalcroze teachers work with a roomful of students. In many cases, you sit among the students and receive the lesson just like they do.

During my first week of Dalcroze training, a local pre-school class was brought in, and my teacher, the late Bob Abramson, did a lesson on the difference between long and short, or staccato and legato. He'd never met or seen this group of children but proceeded to teach a 30-minute class and barely spoke a word. He used piano improvisation and gesture like some kind of wizard. The children responded beautifully. This had an impact not only on the children but also on their teachers (who also took part in the class). One of them pulled Bob aside and told him she was moved by the class and was going to approach her teaching differently as a result. In fact she was so moved, she was reduced to tears.

Dalcroze trainees also move around the room and participate in games and exercises themselves. You're not merely instructed in them—you experience them. There are note-taking sessions and in-depth discussions about what was felt and whether or not it was effective.

Improvisations were critiqued but done in such a way as to allow growth. Once I was asked to improvise a "marching melody" for a class of four-year-olds. I sat at the piano and began playing a bluesy march. Barely eight beats in I was immediately stopped. Mr. Abramson came up to me and said, "Your beats are too tall! These are four-year-olds. They have smaller legs! Play shorter!" I realized I was not thinking of my playing in physical terms.

The solfege lessons were, as described earlier, filled with movement and games. For me, this was an eye-opening experience. We were asked to create a movement-based solfege game on our own and then teach it to the class. Our fellow students assumed the roles of students, and Bob observed us with watchful eyes and (lots of) critique.

In addition to Bob, there were dance and movement teachers. One of these was an expert in the art of gesture and helped us understand how to communicate with students through hand and arm movements while playing the piano.

The training was comprehensive in ways that I truly can't describe on paper. Throughout, I had moments of clarity, and, to this day, I use many of the things I learned on my first day of training. The day I was awarded my Elementary Certificate (which required the teaching of a group of children in front of Bob, the other teachers, and my peers),

I remember Bob standing in front of us that morning. My exam was on my mind, but he began the day by asking a question: "What is your favorite performing art?" Because it was a roomful of musicians, dancers, and actors, the answers were accordingly music, dance, and drama. After a few of these, Bob got a little smile on his face and asked, "Do you know what my favorite performing art is? Teaching."

Dalcroze teachers are trained as artists, and this is because teaching is an art form. Think about the greatest teachers you had as a child and/or all the way through to college. They probably brought some level of artistic quality to their work. Maybe they were a stand-up comic or perhaps a great orator. Maybe they drew beautiful pictures on the chalkboard or in their handouts. Maybe they were great writers. Regardless, they used a creative element to get their subject across and to help you to understand it. In some of these cases, maybe what you remember most about your favorite teacher is how they got you to better understand yourself.

The study of Eurhythmics not only encourages that type of teaching but also trains individuals to be that kind of a teacher. In this modern time of dynamic and developmentally diverse students, Dalcroze teachers are exactly the kind of teachers we need.

5

EURHYTHMICS, THE BRAIN, AND SOCIAL AND EMOTIONAL INTELLIGENCE

Music and Physiology/Music and the Sensory System/
Joseph Can't Jump/Room 2023/"This is stupid . . ."

Jaques-Dalcroze managed to do something that was ahead of his time: Create a method of teaching that focuses on the whole human reaction to music. His creation was a response to what he saw lacking in his students. As a teacher, Dalcroze considered not only his subject but how it could help his students cope with the changes that were taking place not only around them but also within.

Eurhythmics is special in many ways. But perhaps the key thing it does is allow a teacher an approach from multiple perspectives. In essence, it is a dynamic method that utilizes a dynamic art form to teach dynamic individuals.

The ancient Greeks believed knowledge in all of the arts, not just music, inspired thought and curiosity in everything else—politics, science, nature, love—and stimulated us wholly, not singularly. They keyed in on the sensory response to art but also realized how music, specifically, affected all the senses simultaneously. Consider what Plato wrote regarding music education in *The Republic:*

"... *musical training is a more potent instrument
than any other, because rhythm and harmony find
their way into the inward places of the soul, on which
they mightily fasten, imparting grace, and making the
soul of him who is rightly educated graceful ...*"

Aristotle also wrote extensively on the role of music in education, and his thoughts concerning music speak about varied developmental aspects. In *Politics*, Aristotle wrote about how one specific aspect of music, the modes, affect human emotions:

"... *musical modes differ essentially from one another,
and those who hear them are differently affected by
each. Some of them make men sad and grave, like the
so-called Mixolydian; others enfeeble the mind, like the
relaxed modes; another, again, produces a moderate and*

settled temper, which appears to be the peculiar effect of
the Dorian; the Phrygian inspires enthusiasm . . ."

He then goes on further and writes about how another aspect, rhythm, affects character:

"The same principles apply to rhythms; some have a character
of rest, others of motion, and of these latter again, some
have a more vulgar, others a nobler movement. Enough
has been said to show that music has a power of forming
the character and should therefore be introduced into the
education of the young. The study is suited to the stage of
youth, for young persons will not, if they can help, endure
anything which is not sweetened by pleasure, and music has a
natural sweetness. There seems to be in us a sort of affinity to
musical modes and rhythms, which makes some philosophers
say that the soul is a tuning, others, that it possesses tuning."

Aristotle keyed in on the emotional and physical aspects of music and observed how they can help awaken a child to their inner being— awaken them wholly. Dalcroze wrote something similar:

"In my judgment, all of our efforts should be directed to
training our children to become conscious of their personalities,
to develop their temperaments, and to liberate their particular
rhythms of individual life from every trammeling influence."[25]

---

25 Dalcroze p ix (Foreword)

The idea of music as a way not only to "train" students in a singular thing but to simultaneously awaken them from within is not a new idea. It's been around since the beginning of time. In fact, the father of American public education, Horace Mann, wrote:

"Music is a moral means of great efficacy; its practice promotes health; it disarms anger; softens rough and turbulent natures; socializes and brings the whole mind, as it were, into a state of fusion, from which condition the teacher can mold it into what forms he will, as it cools and hardens."[26]

Unfortunately, I believe that we've managed to lose sight of the diverse qualities and depth of music. Instead of viewing music as the dynamic art form it is—like the Greeks and Dalcroze—administrators and music educators have fallen into the (not-so-new) trap of defining a *music class* through the scope of four very narrow lenses: band, chorus, orchestra, or general music class. It is, by and large, viewed as an elective: something that's fun and not necessary to the overall development and education of our children. I see it beyond those and also view it as an untapped resource.

Walk into any American public school and go to the music room, or a music class, and observe what takes place. There may be some singing; the students may be using some drums, rhythm sticks, or other handheld instruments. If you walk into a middle, or high-school band rehearsal, you will find students seated in chairs, plowing

---

26 *The Common School Journal*, by Horace Mann, p 145

through measures of music—and while the students may be aware of the notes and the other students around them, how in tune are they to themselves? Have they been made aware of their own artistic perceptions and abilities? Are they aware of the collaboration that's taking place not just with those around them but within?

Dalcroze said the purpose of Eurhythmics (music) is:

". . . to enable pupils at the end of their course, to say,
not 'I know,' but 'I have experienced,' and so create
in them the desire to express themselves; for the deep
impression of an emotion inspires a longing to communicate
it, to the extent of one's powers, to others."[27]

The words "notes" and "music" are nowhere to be found in that explanation, and Dalcroze is writing as a music educator.

Consider what Dalcroze wrote, and apply it to the developmentally diverse students of today. Now, consider, for a moment, what Dalcroze wrote in the context of modern-day education. Suddenly the way we view education is in the context of professionalism. It's not about curiosity, creativity, or self-discovery. Rather, we currently view education solely as the training of future workers.

Education has, in effect, become about *getting into college* and/or *getting a job*. What matters are tests and class rankings. When you consider the developmentally diverse students now coming to our

---

27 Dalcroze, p 119

schools and how our schools now function and pace themselves, this makes absolutely no sense.

The modern public school model moves at a breakneck pace. There is an enormous amount of stake and importance placed on rankings and tests. This, coupled with an overwhelming message of *everything you do has to have relevance toward the college application process,* flies in the face of the developmentally diverse students who make up our schools.

Is this how we should be educating our kids for their future?

Satya Nadella, the CEO of Microsoft, spoke at the 2017 World Economic Forum in Davos, Switzerland. He was speaking about the job skills needed in a world where technology is changing at a seemingly daily rate and where artificial intelligence (AI) technologies will be much more prevalent. Nadella said of the future and of the skills employees will need:

". . . human values such as common sense and empathy will be scarce. These are the values the citizens of tomorrow need most to make humanity the best that it can be."

The CEO of one of the planet's largest technology companies told a roomful of global financial leaders that, in the rapidly approaching future, the most coveted, in-demand skills have nothing to do with technology. Nadella is essentially saying that, as the future and designing of digital intelligence advance, we must teach emotional and social intelligence.

Consider how much more complex this task is with the developmentally diverse students coming into our schools. Remember: we are emotional beings first. Everything we do—regardless of profession—is shaped by emotions. The job of making sure we are aware of these emotions and using them is a huge part of education. Self-discovery is (I believe) the most crucial piece of education and learning for our kids. Being able to listen to others and being understanding to those around you are also vitally important skills.

In order to move education into the twenty-first century, we must acknowledge the complexity of the integrated and inclusion-based system our schools are a part of. We can't continue to model our teachers, methods, and classrooms—or entire schools—while denying the developmental, social, and economic diversity of our students. It's important to remember that special-needs students, in particular, are, more and more, becoming functional members of society. Understanding what goes into working with them is becoming more important, which means emotional development is an important part of the education process.

Emotions are part of our physical selves. They're not separate from our physiological system but are a byproduct of them. In her book *Eurhythmics for Autism and Other Neurophysiologic Diagnoses*, Dr. Dorita S. Berger points out:

". . . one becomes aware of emotion by way of bodily sensations that become translated, recognized, and defined as feelings."[28]

Dalcroze seemed to be aware of this when he wrote about music education not only in regard to musical training but also in the context

---

28 Berger, p 61

of training of the muscular and nervous systems—our physiology. He believed musical and muscular movement were one and the same. Through his physical and musical games, students learn to embody music and experience their emotions. They relate music not only to the outer world but also, more importantly, to their own inner world. In a Eurhythmics class, students are responding to not only their own feelings and emotions but also to the feelings of those around them. This is vital to overall student development. Again, Dr. Berger:

"Remember that physiological function is individual to each person, according to the manner in which each one's own system has received, perceived, and processed stimuli . . ."[29]

I have taught a roomful of special-needs students who are responding to the physical movements and sounds around them. They are able to exercise emotional responses not just to the music but also to those around them. Mind you, I see the same results when teaching a roomful of typically developing students. The Eurhythmics techniques and games I use carry over.

Dalcroze believed that bodily movements such as gait, walking, running, skipping, and even smaller gestures should be studied as a better way to understand not only music but also the physical and emotional human being creating the music—and he did this for a good reason.

---

29 Berger, p 62

Music's "structure" parallels that of the human body. It travels through space and time—like our biological system. It's no coincidence that musical and biological terms run parallel:

- Space
- Pulse
- Breath
- Air
- Flow

Again, I will let Dr. Berger help make this point:

"Music is temporal energy moving across time and space, the organization and compilation of which is a human invention. What's more, humans created music using fundamentals that the brain and body understand:

- *periodicity: cycles; rhythm; movement*
- *complex frequencies: pitch (melody); timbre; harmony*
- *energy: amplitude of dynamics—volume*
- *structure: form and systems"*[30]

Yes, music is a human invention, but it relies on elements that imitate the movements and cycles of nature that surround us. In essence, music is life.

---

30 Berger, pp 98 and 99

As I touched on earlier, some anthropologists believe music served as a way to bring humans together. It provided a way for early humans to interact socially and emotionally, and to express themselves. It also provided a physical outlet. Some even believe the playing of primitive instruments helped to refine our motor skills, and subsequent chants are what led to speech. There are also theories that say dance evolved from music and that gesture is a byproduct of dance.

Dr. Berger and a colleague, Dr. Daniel J. Schneck—a musician and biomedical engineer—define music as a: "Controlled system of soul processes." They then go on to define the human organism as a "Controlled system of information processing." Both things go through a process involving energy and physical movement, with the final result being an emotional response.

Humans and music both interact with the world around them, and Dalcroze recognized this. Music is not just notes coming out of an instrument. It has energy, feeling, and shape. These attributes are the result of the human beings creating it, and, in order to create music, musicians must understand how to use their bodies to control the energy and feeling that shape the notes and give them emotion.

The similarities between how music and humans interact with the world is extraordinarily similar. Schneck and Berger speak to this point:

"The human body is a controlled system organized in essentially six levels, increasing in size and function, from atoms to molecules, cells, tissues, organs, and systems. Music, too, is a controlled system organized through six basic elements, [also] increasing in size, content, volume, and function—from the smallest structural 'atom' (individual pitches, notes) of a sound idea, to molecules (melodic

'soundscapes,' and harmonic dimensions), functional cells
(phrase and rhythmic units), tissues (timbre, sound quality,
dynamics, and energized textures), organs (combinations
of notes, rhythms, dynamics, phrases, harmonies, timbre,
textures, tonalities that preserve and drive the body of
work), and systems (key structures, modalities, form,
movements, musical styles, variations, etc.)."[31]

Through this statement, you can see the correlation between music and the physical body. Clinical? Yes, but spot on, nonetheless. Choosing to define music modalities as a physical system (like our nervous system) reflects back to what Aristotle noted regarding the modes of music and how they affect us emotionally. It would appear that what Aristotle noted all those thousands of years ago regarding music "forming the character" was quite astute.

Music, like us, moves fast and slow (tempo). Music, like us, translates emotion (dynamics, keys, phrases). Music, like us, interacts kinesthetically with the energy around it (rhythm, meter, beat, dynamics, volume). Humans *respond* to music because we *are* music. Our physical qualities are what shape the music we produce. That music is received by others, and it produces physical, emotional, and social responses.

The Greeks were the first to recognize this, and Dalcroze expanded on it. Advances in science and medicine are now confirming for us that this physical, emotional, social, and neurological interaction does take place. We are also finally beginning to understand why.

---

31 Schneck, Berger, p 33

Consider the amount of sensory input we receive throughout the day:

- Sounds
- Textures
- Smells
- Moving Objects
- Tastes
- Movements of others
- Our own physical movements
- Facial expressions
- Visual symbols

All of this information is processed like this:

Sensory Stimulus ⇨ *Context* ⇨ *Perception* ⇨ *Emotion* ⇨ *Response*

Our responses are shaped by the way we perceive sensory input (energy). This includes not only the loud "BANG!" that wakes you up in the middle of the night but also how your work colleague says "Good morning" to you. Did they say it with a smile? Did they say it with a smile and a gesture? Did they say it with an expression that read *I don't really want to say "Good morning" to you, but I will*?

Our emotions are generated by what we physically feel, see, hear, taste, or smell coming into our body. Our perception shapes it into a response and, being that our individual perceptions are unique, allows for interpretation. The philosopher Susanne Langer refers to this as our "sense data".

Music is energy, and energy vibrates. Our ears (part of our sensory system) pick up this vibration, which is a sensory-based stimulus, and we respond to it. Again, this response is shaped by our perception. A different vibration produces a different perception and, thus, a different response.

As with other sensory input, we respond emotionally to music. The amazing thing is that modern science has shown that musical keys—major (happy) and minor (sad)—are processed in a region of the brain called the medial prefrontal cortex. Scientific opinion regarding the role of that region of the brain varies. Some believe it's responsible for decision-making and long-term memory retrieval. Some believe that, in addition, the medial prefrontal cortex also helps us mark time (days, months, years) and is also key to our emotional development. I find it fascinating that we, as humans, process music in the region of the brain that controls functions specific to learning. This, I believe, is highly relevant when you consider the fact that our public schools now educate more developmentally as well as socially and emotionally challenged students.

I also believe that the advances in science and medicine have just begun to scratch the surface regarding what music can accomplish from the perspective of emotional, social, and physical development. Consider this in the context of the emerging field of immunotherapy. This is a medical protocol that utilizes the body's own immune system to fight serious illnesses. We've known the immune system is extraordinarily powerful, but now we're beginning to realize *how* powerful and how we can harness that power.

Scientific, medical, and technological advances have allowed for thorough and more in-depth ways of looking at our immune system. I believe the same has happened with how music affects our bodies. A 2013 study at University of Connecticut focused on movement based music therapies specifically for children on the Autism spectrum. In the opening to the paper published, the researchers state:

"The rising incidence of Autism Spectrum Disorders (ASDs)
has led to a surge in the number of children needing autism

interventions. This paper is a call to clinicians to diversify autism interventions and to promote the use of embodied music-based approaches to facilitate multisystem development."

The paper continues:

"Musical training impacts various forms of development including communication, social-emotional, and motor development in children with ASDs and other developmental disorders as well as typically developing children. In this review, we will highlight the multisystem impairments of ASDs, explain why music and movement therapies are a powerful clinical tool, as well as describe mechanisms and offer evidence in support of music therapies for children with ASDs."[32]

Dalcroze developed Eurhythmics from a dynamic approach. Much of what he created was done from a perspective that is not necessarily musical. He, like the reseracers at University of Connecticut as well as Doctors Schneck and Berger, looked at music from a physiological perspective. So much of Eurhythmics comes from someone who was considering the nervous system and the mind/body connection while developing a teaching method.

As our public-school populations expand to accommodate more and more students with special needs and/or classifications, and the

_____

32 Srinivasan, Sudha M. and Bhat, Anjana N., "A Review of "Music and Movement" erapies for Children with Autism: Embodied Interventions for Multisystem Development" (2013). p://digitalcommons.uconn.edu/libr_oa/13

world around us continues to change and affect our kids, perhaps it is necessary to consider bringing in teachers trained in a method that was developed by someone who wrote:

"Presently, however, a study of the reactions produced by piano-playing, in parts of the body other than the hands— movements with the feet, oscillations in the trunk, and head, a swaying of the whole body, etc.—led me to the discovery that musical sensations of a rhythmic nature call for the muscular and nervous response of the <u>whole organism</u> [my emphasis]. I set my pupils' exercises in stepping and halting, and trained them to react physically to the perception of musical rhythms."[33]

Music may be a singular art form, but I believe it can be used in the most dynamic fashion regarding the whole education of our kids.

The great philosopher and thinker Susanne Langer wrote extensively on the role the arts play in education and how they help to develop our senses. You can hear echoes of Dalcroze in Langer's book *Philosophy in a New Key*:

"The nervous system is the organ of the mind; its center is the brain, its extremities the sense-organs; and any characteristic function it may possess must govern the

---

33 Dalcroze, p vi (Foreword)

work of all its parts. In other words, the activity of our senses is 'mental' not only when it reaches the brain, but in its very inception, whenever the alien world outside impinges on the furthest and smallest receptor."[34]

How great is it that Langer defines the nervous system as "the organ of the mind." I think Dalcroze would've agreed with that definition, as that was the focus of his method. In fact, one thing Langer refers to a lot in *Philosophy in a New Key* is what she calls "aesthetic emotion." She is defining how we respond to art, and I think this is what Dalcroze saw as an essential piece to learning.

The word "aesthetic" is one not commonly used to define education or the learning process. An aesthetic experience is feeling the connection of the senses—one between the neurological and the physical. This is a key element of Eurhythmics. Dalcroze did not think of mind and body as separate, but he knew they had to work together. He saw how music—and the response it created—was capable of bringing that out in his students.

Dalcroze saw how emotions were the byproduct of what we feel through our senses. His games and exercises stimulate the "organ of the mind" and allow for a truly aesthetic learning experience. This is why Eurhythmics is a method that can not only awaken students artistically and physically but can also bring them together socially, emotionally, intellectually, and aesthetically.

As I said at the beginning of this book, I believe education is a journey of self-discovery. This sentiment is paraphrased by Eliot Eisner,

---

34 Langer, p 73

who, in his book *Arts and the Creation of Mind*, defined education as "The process of learning how to invent yourself." Education, in other words, is not just facts and figures. I also believe we have begun realizing this truth more in the wake of the COVID-19 pandemic and the subsequent closing of schools. It wasn't solely the live instruction our kids missed, but the social and emotional connections they make with their peers as well as teachers.

When we awaken physically, emotionally, socially, and aesthetically, this helps to awaken us intellectually as well. I had an experience with this process that I will never forget; it helped me to understand even more how we all learn through the body.

I teach in a self-contained school for autistic children that serves ages Pre-Kindergarten to middle school. Autism-spectrum disorders present a wide range of symptoms and attributes that vary from individual to individual, which is both wonderful and challenging.

Some of my students are non-verbal; others suffer from low muscle tone. Some have social and/or behavioral complications. As teachers and aides, we have to find a "road in," and, in many cases, use an attribute of ASD to help us.

A few years ago, I had a student, "Joseph,"[35] who was a mid-level functioning student. While he had a significant speech delay, he was able to manage some language but suffered an array of sensory delays as well as some low muscle tone. He slumped when he walked, and one of the OTs at school told me that Joseph did not enjoy their sessions together.

One day I had planned to do a game with my students that involved jumping through colored circles in time with a rhythmic melody I played on the piano. The rhythm I used was a basic dotted quarter note, eighth note structure (like the old song "Tea for Two"). I would get each student to stand on a start line, tell them to wait for the music,

---

35 Not his real name.

count it off, and then say "GO!" As the student jumped through the circles, the rest of the class would sing the colors in that rhythm.

When it was Joseph's turn, one of the aides said to me, "I don't think he should do this." "Why not?" I asked.

"Joseph can't jump," came her response.

I had observed Joseph moving in my classes and knew he was capable of responding physically to music, albeit with small movements. After some cajoling, I got the aide to help him over to the start line. At first, I asked him to just move to my piano playing and improvised a short little tune. I also asked him to bend his knees as best he could as he moved.

After about a minute, I stopped my improvisation. I yelled "GO!" and began playing the rhythm I had been playing for the other students. To everyone's shock, Joseph not only jumped into the first circle but kept going through all of them. We couldn't believe it.

At the end, Joseph was smiling and, we could tell, was quite proud of himself. His teacher came up to me later to tell me how, for the rest of the day, Joseph was much more alert and aware in the classroom in ways she'd never seen. It seemed like the game and the music had woken him up a bit.

That day showed me more than ever how a Eurhythmics game could help awaken students to their abilities. I will never forget the smile on Joseph's face. It wasn't so much about the physical accomplishment but about his emotional response. It really was a great thing to see.

When I reflect on that moment, I often think about how rhythm and melody, and watching his classmates, allowed Joseph the ability to move along with something and not just *hear* the music but *feel* it in his body. Occupational therapists use the term "organize" when they allow a child or student of theirs to jump for a minute. The rhythm of the jumping allows them to put timing into their physiology and set them up for activity. I think my improvisation—and the movement it inspired—helped to organize Joseph for the jumping.

This, I believe, is why Eurhythmics can be used for classroom settings outside of music. In modern classrooms, different classifications present different challenges for teachers. Oftentimes these challenges can create struggles within the group not only for the students but for the teachers as well. Suddenly the needs of one student become the priority of the entire class. A teacher may feel like she/he is spending all of their time and energy with that one student and may begin to feel conflicted.

A situation like this could also create animosity among the other students. They could begin to feel neglected. I have friends who are teachers who have told me they have a student in class with a diagnosis who requires a lot of one on one time as well as attention. They have subsequently seen typically developing students begin mirroring the behaviors of the classified student just to get attention themselves. Something like this speaks to the delicate balance of the classroom dynamic. Creating that balance—and a mindset that essentially says, "It's not about *you*; it's not about *me*—it's about *we*" can be very difficult. In fact, I would say this is the essence of teaching.

One of the worst things that can happen in a classroom is a "power struggle." This is when a student, or students, do not want to adhere to the rules or be a part of the group—or they may have a classification that doesn't allow for this. They want to operate separate from the rest of the students. While there is individual work involved in any classroom, the ability to be part of a class is essential to overall learning as well as the daily functionality of the classroom.

When I present staff-development workshops, I ask teachers about some of their biggest challenges, and, more often than not, they share stories of having to deal with taking a classroom of students and getting them to work as one. In many instances, there's a power struggle involved in the process. It could be small or large, but attempting to get students to come together as one is no easy task.

A single student can throw off the dynamic of an entire classroom. I have witnessed an individual student throw off the dynamic of an *entire school*. For many students, becoming part of the group is a very difficult process and concept to understand. Again, I go back to the great basketball coach John Wooden. He was able to accomplish so much because he believed in making sure his players were acknowledged for their individual talents. But he also made sure to remind them how individual talents contribute to the team as a whole (putting on your socks and shoes). This is what teaching is.

Teaching young people the ability to move and flow within a class is probably one of the most essential pieces to learning. If a teacher doesn't have a healthy class dynamic—how can they teach anything?

I had an experience with a power struggle that, to this day, serves as a reminder and a lesson for me.

One of my most influential—and most challenging—teaching experiences involved working at an inner-city public school in Newark, New Jersey. The school where I taught serves grades K-8 and is located in one of the toughest parts of the city. Many of the children I taught were growing up in significant to severe poverty. Directly behind the school is one of the more notorious public housing projects, where many of my students lived. While I was there, the community around the school was also experiencing a significant amount of gang violence.

It was a difficult environment to teach in because so many of the children were completely unaware of their potential. I realized this my first day at the school—although this realization was not whole. I had made the mistake of thinking I understood what life in a poor, inner-city community was like. In fact, I'd soon discover, I had no idea.

I had been hired about two months into the school year, so the students had already developed a sense of routine, and I was going to be new to that routine.

The morning of my first day, I was in the music room, looking over my lesson plans, student rosters, and other materials. There was a quiet knock on the door, and I turned to see a 6'3" bear of a man with a shaved head standing in my room. He extended his hand and introduced himself. He was James[36], the gym teacher.

After some introductions and small talk, James looked down at my desk, and then he looked up at me with a furrowed brow and said, "I see you have room 2023 for your first class."

"Yup, first one of the day."

"I'm just going to tell you straight: 2023 are the toughest class in the school. They're very difficult to control."

After glancing down at my desk, I said; "They're third-graders . . . how tough could they be?"

That's when James—all 6'3" and 200-plus pounds of him—looked me square in the eye and answered, "I have 2023 on Wednesdays, and I don't sleep Tuesday nights."

After a few more minutes of conversation, James left. With his words echoing in my head, I took the last moments of my morning to further prepare myself. I reviewed my lesson plans, tried some improvisations on the piano, and ran through possible scenarios in my head. Having spent the previous five years teaching at a school for autistic students, I'd had many unique classroom experiences. What could I possibly see here in Newark that was much different?

About twenty minutes later, the bell rang, and the students of 2023 did not so much enter the music room—they *engulfed* it. Before I could do anything, the room erupted into literal chaos.

---

36 Not his real name.

The students ran around the room, ran past me, and behind me. I went to the piano and began improvising something in an effort to gain their attention. Five students ran up to the piano and began banging on it and laughing. Before I could say anything, a school security guard appeared in my room with two boys and said in an (rightfully) angry tone; "These two ran out of your class! Keep an eye on your students!"

I had no idea they'd even left.

Something flew past my head and hit the wall behind me. I turned to see that a few students had somehow gotten my closets open and were now throwing things around the room. These included crayons, as well as small instruments like woodblocks and finger cymbals. A girl standing in front of me began crying. The room was out of control, and I began doing something that I'd never done to students before: yelling and screaming like a maniac.

I wasn't just taken out of my comfort zone—I was *ripped* from it. My classroom was now unsafe. I waded into the fray and grabbed crayons and instruments from students. I turned just in time to see three boys heading toward the door. I ran up and asked where they were going. "We're leaving" one boy casually answered. "No, you're not" came my response. That's when one of the boys—who, again, was in *third grade*—looked me square in the eye and cursed me out in a way I'd never been cursed out before, and he used *every word* imaginable!

By the end of the class (in which nothing of substance was accomplished), I was a sweaty, red-faced mess. I had spent the last fifteen minutes of class literally screaming. The students laughed at me, and this was primarily because kids are smart. They recognized that I'm not a screamer, and this frustrated me even more.

My first class in Newark was a disaster of epic proportions on a scale I do not wish upon any teacher—or any individual, for that matter. I will never forget it as long as I live. While room 2023 was the toughest class, I quickly discovered that almost every other class was similar. Soon, I began to realize that, while the kids were testing me to some extent, they were also coming from an environment I didn't understand. Instead of trying to learn about the environment and the children themselves, I spent my first month in Newark screaming like a lunatic and accomplishing nothing.

Before long, I wasn't sleeping not only on Sunday nights—because I knew 2023 were coming Monday morning—but I wasn't sleeping *Sunday through Thursday.* That's when my wife, Laura, said to me, "You either have to change up your approach, or you need to quit. If you don't do either of those, you're going to make yourself sick."

I spent one entire Sunday taking a step back, reevaluating my approach but also thinking about the kids themselves. I had gone into Newark in a very selfish mindset. I thought about the kids and their situation. Then, I reflected upon my (forgotten) Dalcroze studies and came up with a plan that I thought would allow me to teach.

The thing I first had to come to terms with was that a single student in 2023 ran the class: Tanya[37]. This was a humbling experience, as it took self-recognition to understand that I had no say—or control—over the current dynamic of that class. All of the other kids listened to Tanya. Whatever she said, the others did. She was in charge. This really frustrated me because Tanya's word was stronger than mine, but the Sunday I spent reflecting caused me to realize my frustration with her was my big mistake.

One of the best lessons my Eurhythmics teacher, Bob Abramson, taught me was to be alert for the gifts students bring to class every day. He told me the gifts may not always be shiny and could come in the form of harsh reminders. This made me realize that, instead of being frustrated with Tanya, I needed to see her as something nobody had

---

37 Not her real name.

probably ever seen her as: a natural leader. I would use her natural leadership to help me. This became the essence of my strategy.

In addition, the kids in 2023 (and the rest of the school) were unaware that I played the drums. Before becoming a music teacher, I actually worked as a touring, professional drummer for years. That Monday, I brought a small drum set to school and set it up behind the piano—out of view from the students. My drums were going to act as the catalyst for organizing room 2023 . . . I hoped.

When the bell rang that morning, room 2023 ran into the room, and . . . the chaos began. I let them run around for a minute. Then I strolled over to the drum set and began playing a hip-hop type beat.

The chaos didn't just stop—it *halted*. Suddenly, for the first time since I'd entered the school, there was silence in my classroom. Before anyone could say a word, Tanya yelled, "Do that again!"

I looked at her with a smile and calmly answered, "No. Not until everyone sits down." To my surprise (and relief), Tanya turned to the class and yelled, *"Everyone sit down!"*

And they did!

Then Tanya turned to me and said, "Play it again."

I, again, casually (and with a smile on face) answered, "No," but, this time, I followed that with, "You didn't say *please*." Tanya looked at me and asked her question again, this time prefacing it: *"Please* play it again." Much to her surprise, I smiled, answered "No," and then said, "Now *you* have to sit down." Tanya smiled back at me[38]; then she walked over to a chair and sat down. Instead of confronting her, I'd turned the whole thing into a game, but one that used her skills as well as mine.

The window had opened, and that's when I began a basic Eurhythmics lesson with the class. I gestured to them—I didn't speak—that when I began playing the drums, they had to clap, but

---

38 !

when I stopped, they had to stop. Of course, as soon as I began playing the beat, a group of kids stood up and started dancing and running around the room. I not only stopped but began picking up the drums to put them away. Tanya stood up and yelled at the students to sit down—and they sat down.

My strategy was working: Tanya had become my teaching assistant!

Once the students were back in their seats, I began playing the drums. They clapped along until I stopped. When I started, they began clapping again. Eventually I added the quick-reaction elements. At the next stop, I waited longer. I could see the anticipation in the kid's faces as they waited for me to start. Some were trying not to laugh, and some even had their eyes closed. Some were looking at me with their hands up, eyes open, and smiling with an open-mouthed excitement. I began playing but stopped almost immediately. This made them laugh out loud.

What the kids in room 2023 didn't realize was that they were now *listening to me*. They were following my instructions. I had begun to create the student/teacher dynamic through my subject. Instead of screaming at them to sit down and listen, I played a game that allowed them to discover that they were actually capable of doing it—and I used one of their peers to help me.

As we progressed, I added other elements. I asked them to stand up—which showed that I now trusted them not to run around the room. I then had them keep clapping when I stopped—to show me they could hold the beat.

At the last stop, I walked out from behind the drum set and asked if they liked the game. They all answered "Yes." Then I told them I was very proud of them because, while the game is fun, it's also very hard. One student said it wasn't hard, but then I explained how the game required them not only to listen but also to be good musicians (they had to stay in time with me). They also had to listen to, and watch, *each other*. In other words, I told them, we all had to work together—like a band or an orchestra.

I asked them if, the next time they came to music, they would like to play another game, and they shook their heads "Yes." Just then, their teacher came into the music room to bring them back to class. Before anyone could move, I ran back behind the drums and began playing a marching rhythm. They all marched to their teacher and out the door. Some of the kids smiled and waved to me.

Then I collapsed on the floor!

For the rest of the fall and most of the winter, I did not do any traditional "music classes" with any of my students in Newark. I used Eurhythmics-based games and exercises to build a class dynamic as well as relationships with my kids. In fact, I built off the start/stop model and began meeting classes in the hallway with a small hand drum. I would play a soft beat and have them walk to my classroom with my rhythm, and stop/start along the way. It helped to organize them and get them set before we even got into the room.

The other thing that helped tremendously was that Newark has dance as part of their curriculum. Right next to my music room was the dance studio, and the dance teacher, Janelle, was a godsend. She is the best teacher I've ever seen in my life, and she helped me in ways that I'll forever be grateful for. She told me many of the kids' stories and gave me insight into a lot of their experiences. We also began doing things together—collaborating and creating inter-disciplinary lessons. We, along with the visual-arts teacher, created a Black History Month concert that was one of the best things I've ever been a part of.

Through all of this, as well as the physical and musical movement of Eurhythmics, I saw my students begin to understand how to work together. Through the games we played, I gained insight into which students were going to struggle physically, socially, or emotionally—or all three. This, in turn, allowed me to reach out to those students individually and begin building relationships with them.

Using Eurhythmics to help my students awaken physically and emotionally, I now feel, could be a vital tool in today's developmentally diverse classrooms. Awakening students to their social and emotional potential is a vital step in bringing students together as a class. Dalcroze was a visionary when it came to this. You can see and understand this when he wrote:

"[Students] should be enlightened as to the relations existing between soul and mind, between the conscious and the subconscious, between imagination and the process of action. Thoughts should be brought into immediate contact with behavior."[39]

Learning is not just a process of solving problems or a score on a test. It is awakening to the abilities that the process—whatever it is—may require. Learning presents an array of speed bumps and/or roadblocks that are in no way limited to those within academic subjects. Learning also includes solving problems related to social and emotional development, which, for many students, stands in the way of their intellectual growth and development. As our school populations have expanded developmentally, this aspect is becoming more complex.

---

39 Dalcroze, p ix (Foreword)

What happened with my students in room 2023, I define as *aesthetic learning*. Eurhythmics allowed the students a different experience and a way to perceive what they were capable of. *Perception* is defined as: "The state of or process of becoming aware of something through the senses." It's also defined as: "A way of regarding, understanding, or interpreting something; a mental impression."

Eurhythmics allowed an opening of self-perception in my students—an awakening through the senses. The problem of understanding how to interact with others and with me, individually, was addressed aesthetically. It allowed the act of learning to take on an artistic experience.

Dalcroze wrote about this type of emotional awakening in the classroom:

*"Aesthetic emotion is a product of the refinement
of the senses, susceptibility of the nervous
system, and mental flexibility."*[40]

Regarding the same idea, John Dewey—a contemporary of Dalcroze—wrote in his essay "Art as Experience":

*". . . a problem receives its solution; a game is played
through; a situation, whether that of eating a meal,*

---

40   Dalcroze, pp 174 and 175

playing a game of chess, carrying on a conversation,
writing a book, or taking part in a political campaign,
is so rounded out that its close is a consummation
and not a cessation. Such an experience is a whole
and carries with it its own individualizing quality
and self-sufficiency. It is an experience."[41]

Dewey defines a problem as an experience, and one that requires not just a solution but an awakening. Again, learning is the process of awakening to the abilities that solving the problem may require.

Teachers now face classrooms filled with developmentally diverse students who have dynamic individual needs—multiple abilities. A classroom filled with all typically developing children presents challenges in awakening them to their abilities and bringing them together. Imagine a developmentally diverse classroom, like today's.

Dalcroze wrote how Eurhythmics was able to awaken students to the "marvelous mechanics of their body . . ." and through this, students would be able to:

". . . experience a growing yearning to make full use of
the abundant forces in his control. His imagination will
likewise develop as his mind, released from all constraint and
nerves disquietude, gives full rein to his [imagination]."

41 John Dewey, "Art as Experience," p 39

Dalcroze is describing an awakening that begins in the body and the mind simultaneously. He continues:

> *"Functioning develops the organ, and the consciousness of organic functioning develops thought. And as the child feels himself delivered from all physical embarrassment and mental obsession of lower order, added to the sense— acquired by the practice of <u>combining his individual efforts with those of the rest of the class</u> [my emphasis]— . . . he will conceive a profound joy, of an elevated character, a new factor in ethical progress, a new stimulus to willpower."*[42]

The organ Dalcroze speaks of is the nervous system. This system opens the mind and awakens students not only individually but also to how their individual talents and insights contribute to the class as a whole.

A class that can move together can work together. I saw this with my students in room 2023, as well as with the rest of the kids in Newark that year. Mind you, this was not a smooth practice by any stretch of the imagination. It took an extraordinary amount of time and work, and there were many bumps along the way. But I am proud to say that I witnessed many students suddenly awaken to their social, emotional, and intellectual capabilities.

I'm going to wrap this anecdote up by telling you that my year in Newark culminated with me bringing the kids from room 2023 to a youth orchestra festival sponsored by the New Jersey Symphony

---

42 Dalcroze, pp 174–175

Orchestra. Seeing them play that day with their peers is something I never imagined. If you had asked me that first day, I would've never thought we'd have gotten to that point. I was so proud of them. The road to that moment was challenging, but it was Eurhythmics that allowed me to do it. The exercises and games I did in class allowed the students—and me—to see what they were truly capable of.

After my year in Newark ended, I eventually returned to my old district and began working with a wide array of student populations. One of the schools I began working in was an alternative high school for at-risk inner-city students.

Not many people are familiar with alternative education in the United States. These are schools designed for students who are at risk of not finishing their schooling by the age of 21 (which is when American students age out of the public education system). These students are labeled as "at risk" for a number of reasons, many of which are related to their socioeconomic status and/or emotional problems they may be suffering. Alternative education is designed to address these students and give them an alternative way to meet their requirements and graduate.

Alternative education is a significant piece of the American public-school landscape. A 2010 study done by the National Center for Educational Statistics found that 646,500 kids are enrolled in alternative education schools nationwide[43]. With nearly one million American kids in these programs, it's obvious they're highly relevant to American education as a whole.

The students I was teaching were very similar to those I'd taught in Newark. Many were coming to school out of poverty and/or difficult home lives. Many got off the bus after school and went straight to a

---

43 "Alternative Schools and Programs for Public School Students at Risk of Educational Failure: 2007–2008 First Look" March 2010 by Priscilla Rouse Carver Laurie Lewis, Westat and Peter Tice National Center for Education Statistics

job of some kind. There were many students who had emotional issues as a result of their home lives. Some had emotional issues because they had been abused.

I had not experienced this specific type of environment, and, while Newark had prepared me for a lot of what I saw, some of what I experienced was new. I had many students who were gay and, as a result, had been abused or bullied in their district high school. I had students who announced they were pregnant at some point during the year. There were a number of boys who were flirting with gang life. Still, the most shocking thing to me was how so many of the kids were living in extreme poverty.

Right as the year started, I let the principal know I was interested in applying for a grant to rent some violins. I felt getting the students to learn an instrument could help with their sense of accomplishment as well as guide them toward recognizing their potential.

Before I could accomplish that, however, I had to see what I was working with. These students were all new for me. I didn't know them, and they didn't know me. This environment would be different not only because of the students' emotional state but also because of their wide age range. I would have classes in which the student age range was literally 16–20. Many of the kids were behind on their schoolwork because of their jobs. Some had failed so many classes in their district high school that they were now in our school as a result. We also had kids who experienced legal problems that affected their schoolwork.

On my first day I could not help but flash back to my experience with room 2023. There was no way I was going to allow a situation like that to occur, so I planned on beginning my class with a Eurhythmics game right out of the gate.

One of the games I had been shown by Bob Abramson involved having students pass a beanbag or piece of crumpled paper from hand to hand in time with an improvised piano tune. I thought this would be a great place to start because it would allow me to observe physical movement as well as personalities and even musical capabilities.

I walked into the room and, as I set up my keyboard, began telling the students about my background and where I was coming from. I then wrote my list on the board:

Music:

1. See It
2. Hear It
3. Speak/Sing It
4. Move It
5. Feel It

I turned to see a bunch of puzzled, disinterested faces—as expected. That's when I asked them to stand up; then I walked around and handed them each a small beanbag. These kids were all looking at me like I was crazy. I explained that I was going to play the piano and that they would have to pass the beanbag from hand to hand in time with my playing. There were many eye rolls (of course), but once I began playing, I noticed many of the eye-rollers were moving, passing, *and* smiling.

After a few rounds, I made the students partner up. Now there were two students, with one beanbag between them, facing one another. I explained how they would have to pass the beanbag to each other, with the first student going from right to left and then passing over to their partner's right, opposite them. Then the partner would pass it to their left, and then back. This would all be in time with the music.

I told them how they had to not only listen to my music and the beat but also make good passes. They would have to watch and move with their partner. In other words, they would have to work together.

After a few rounds of this, one student spoke up and said, "This is the stupidest thing I've ever done." I looked over to see a tall young man shaking his head. "Why is it stupid, and what is your name?" I asked him.

"It's boring, and my name is Tyrell."[44]

I had my class assistant!

"Well, Tyrell, the objective is to eventually be able to pass the beanbag around a circle that is made up of the entire class. But I don't think you can do that now. That takes time and practice."

"We can do it," came his reply.

"It takes a lot of listening and focus; plus, you have to be able to work with and help each other."

"What do we get if we do it?"

This was an opening I was hoping for. What Tyrell didn't understand was just how difficult a game this really was. I was about to extend a challenge that, when you read it, will sound like an absolutely insane proposition from a teacher. The first thing I did was arrange all the students into one big circle in the classroom. Then I told them what was going to happen.

Standing in the middle of the circle, I began to talk to them: "OK, I'll tell you what. You have to get the beanbag around the circle one time, but you can't lose the beat, you can't drop the beanbag, and, if you drop it, you can't curse."

There was a round of very overconfident laughter. "That's way easy," Tyrell said. "What do we get when we do it?"

"If you can get the beanbag around the circle on the first try, without losing the beat, dropping it, or cursing at each other, for the rest of the school year, every time you come to class, we'll watch movies, and I'll bring donuts."

---

44 Not his real name.

The looks on my new students' faces were a combination of shock and expressions that read, *This guy's nuts.* There were some confident chuckles, and Tyrell could not ask for the beanbag fast enough.

"Do you want to practice passing one time?" I asked.

"Hell, no! We don't need to do that!" said one cocky student. "Just start playing your piano!"

"OK, but remember," I said as I pointed to what I'd written on the board, "music is not just one thing. It's not just the beat. It's watching, listening, and moving with your classmates and bandmates. It's a lot of things at the same time."

"We've got this!" came the confident voice of Tyrell.

"Alright. When I say 'go,' the music will start, and so will the passing. One, two, ready, go!"

The class was composed of seventeen students in the circle, and the beanbag didn't get past the fourth one. It was on the floor. I stopped the music. A few students threw their hands up in the air in annoyed frustration, but before they could open their mouths, I said with a smile, "Remember, no cursing."

They begged me for another chance. I agreed but said, "You may want to talk a bit first. What went wrong? Why did you drop the beanbag? Are you all watching each other? Are you focused? How's the passing?"

"Just start playing again!" came a confident voice from the circle.

The second time, they got further. The beanbag made it to the sixth student and then dropped to the floor. I couldn't interject in time. A huge "Ohhhh!" went up from the circle. Tyrell was pacing around, and before I could say anything, some yelling, finger pointing . . . and cursing started.

I managed to quiet the class down and walked back into the middle of the circle. "Do you see how hard it is to work together? Not as easy as you thought, right? This ridiculous and silly game is harder than you think because it's so many things at the same time, just like music. Instead of yelling, why don't you think about why you couldn't do it? What went wrong? Did your classmates drop the beanbag because of the way it was passed or the way it was received? Maybe the person next to you dropped the beanbag because of *you*? Should you all pass the same way? Were some people moving other body parts while passing? Were you all moving in time? There's a lot to think about."

The best part was that the students were all listening to me. In fact, it was so quiet in the room that a security guard stuck her head in to see what was going on. I had the students attention, and I used it to explain how this beanbag game was a way to show them how they were going to have to learn to use their hands, arms, and bodies to play the violin. They were also going to have to learn to listen and focus, not just on what *they* were playing but also on what their *classmates* were playing.

Before the bell rang, Tyrell asked, "Can you give us one more chance on the game next time?"

It was a great first start, and—again—Eurhythmics had helped me establish it. I had used physical movement (and donuts) to help the kids understand what was involved in becoming a group. I didn't have them sit in chairs and explain it to them. I let them feel it for themselves. They now had an idea of what our class was going to be.

The use of Eurhythmics intrigued the kids. I caught a lot of students secretly enjoying the beanbag game—despite their age. I think it allowed them to open up a little bit and not just feel the music but express and enjoy themselves. These tough kids were actually able to drop their guard—something they weren't used to—and laugh a little. I wondered how much they would smile the rest of that week. How much joy did my new students experience on a regular basis?

"Joy" is a word that we rarely use when we speak of learning or a classroom experience. Dalcroze, however, used it quite often and wrote about the importance of joy in the classroom:

"Joy arises in the child the moment his faculties are liberated from any restraint, and he becomes conscious of his control over them, and decides on the direction in which that control shall be exercised. This joy is the product of a joint sense of emancipation and responsibility, comprising a vision of our creative potentialities, a balance of natural forces, and a rhythmic harmony of desires and powers."[45]

The feeling of joy is an awakening. Imagine being able to come into a classroom and feel liberated? Yes, I sound a bit idealistic, but that's how we need to think today. Our classrooms are so developmentally, socially, and emotionally diverse that we need to have teachers in them who can take dynamic approaches to teaching. Eurhythmics allows students and teachers to see what their capabilities are.

I used the beanbag lesson plan for the rest of my classes that first day and I got mixed results. In one class, the students were laughing so hard, the security guard ran in *again*. In another class, the students were generally disinterested. It was a mixed bag of responses and results. But the game allowed me, as a teacher, to see what I would be working with.

By the end of the day, I was better able to understand which classes would be more challenging than others. I'd made notes on students who were apprehensive or shy. I also made notes on students who were the opposite of that (like Tyrell). I could also observe hand movements and

---

45 Dalcroze, p 175

see who may have had some difficulties there. As a teacher—and not just of music—you discover a lot about the dynamics and makeup of a room when you ask the students to move together. This is something I believe we need to embrace as the education of kids continues to evolve.

Maybe it's time to begin classes with the words, "OK, everyone—stand up!" instead of "Everyone needs to sit down." Beginning a class—or a school year, for that matter—with a movement-based game or exercise will provide teachers with an insight into the dynamics of their students they would not see otherwise. Dalcroze was, perhaps, thinking this when he wrote, in 1921:

"The education of tomorrow must embrace reconstruction preparation, and adaptation: aiming, on the one hand, at the re-education of the nervous faculties and the attainment of mental calm and concentration . . ."[46]

An expansion on this idea is where I see music education as a whole playing a much larger role in American public education. Music—specifically Eurhythmics—should be used to help teachers as well as administrators better understand the dynamic students they must now teach. I see it as a way to move all of education further into the twenty-first century.

---

46 Dalcroze, p viii (Foreword)

6

THE NEW MUSIC EDUCATION

*Eurhythmics Training for non-Music Teachers/The Floating
Eurhythmics Teacher/The Teachers Collective*

I spent the year between my teaching in Newark and returning to my old school district, working as a substitute teacher in my hometown school district. While I put myself down to work in music classes, the district picked up on my special-needs experience and would often place me to sub in self-contained classes of special-needs students or even in resource rooms. I had one experience while working as a sub that helped shine a light on many of the changes I am writing about.

On this particular day I was working in a self-contained room for autistic students. When I arrived for the day, I was looking at the teacher's instructions and noticed that the students had music class in the later part of the morning. When I brought the kids down for music, I asked the teacher if he would mind if I remained during class, and he was actually thrilled with the idea. I did not tell him that I was a music teacher. I wanted to truly observe what he did and thought it would be best for me to do so in the capacity of just a sub.

The class began, and, right away, I was surprised. As anyone who has worked with autistic students knows, moving them out of their regular classroom presents challenges. There's a lot in play: The students leave their regular classroom, walk down the hall, and enter a new space. There is now a period of readjustment. The chairs in the music room were different from those in the regular classroom, and they were arranged in a different order. There was a carpet on the floor, whereas the regular classroom had none. In addition to a piano, there were loose instruments scattered about the room that the students all wanted to pick up, touch, and/or play with.

The first thing the music teacher did was spend about ten minutes asking the students to sit down and to stop talking. The one thing that surprised me was that he did not use the piano to help him accomplish this. Rather, he stood in front of the room and clapped his hands (loudly) in an effort to get the students' attention.

I also noticed one student was shielding his eyes. Oftentimes, autistic children have heightened sensitivity to light and/or sound. The lighting in the regular classroom was a bit lower than the music room, and I could see how this affected him. There was one student who kept trying to ask the music teacher a question (something to do with music from *The Muppet Movie*), but the teacher seemed frazzled and more concerned with, again, trying to get everyone to sit down.

When all of the students were finally in their seats, he began to play something on the piano. Suddenly, the boy who had been shielding his eyes also began covering his ears and yelling. The music teacher stopped abruptly. I don't think he knew why the boy was yelling and seemed angry about it.

When the class ended, the aides (who also stayed in the music room) began lining the kids up. I went over to the music teacher and asked if he was OK. While shaking his head, he answered in a harried voice, "I just don't know what to do with them."

I must tell you right away that this anecdote is not meant to disparage the music teacher. I genuinely felt bad for him. In fact, I had flashbacks to my experience with room 2023 in Newark. Why didn't I step in? Because I wanted to see how it all played out. I truly wanted to understand how, or if, he knew how to work with a roomful of autistic students.

Music is a form that should be viewed as an asset to a self-contained class of autistic students, and not something that presents a struggle. Here was a room that could be used in a capacity to wake the kids up and help organize them physically, socially, and emotionally for the rest of the day, and it was not that at all.

Later that day, I went down to the music room and confessed. I told the music teacher of my experience and asked if he had received any training for working with special-needs kids. "Very little," came his reply. He told me he'd been teaching for twenty-five years and had seen the student population change in the school. Despite this, he never received any updates to his training or understanding of these diverse students. I then asked if he was open to some ideas and suggestions. He jumped up and grabbed a notebook.

I began by telling him he should turn off one row of his classroom lights when he knew that class was coming in. When I explained about heightened sensitivity, he shook his head and said, "No one ever told me that." I also told him that he should play his piano at a very low volume for the same reason.

I then showed him a few games that involved piano improvisation connected to bodily movements. He was jotting stuff in his notebook but would pause me for questions. I told him of my time in a self-contained school of autistic kids but then began telling him of my Eurhythmics training. I asked if he'd had any Eurhythmics in college, and, while he knew what it was, he had very little knowledge of the method as a whole.

After a few more minutes, we had to stop because he had a class coming in, but he asked if I could come back at the end of the day. I was glad to do so, and we spent the afternoon in his room. I showed him some more games and ideas that I'd used, and he peppered me with questions. After about an hour and a half, I had to go but told him I'd be glad to help him any way I could. He thanked me and, while shaking my hand, said, "I don't understand why they don't update us on this. It doesn't make any sense."

I came away that day asking, "Do music teachers receive any training specific to working with autistic children? How could a veteran teacher receive nothing specific to this population of students?" If anyone had witnessed the change in school populations, it was twenty-five-year veterans like himself.

Recently, I was speaking with a friend who's an aide to a fifth-grade autistic boy in an inclusion class. This means he's mainstreamed in a class of typically developing students. I asked if they had music class, and she told me how the teacher was "clueless" when it came to the needs of her student. Her student had a sensitivity to loud sounds, and she told me that the teacher (who had a lovely singing voice) sings at top volume. This made her student upset, and she typically had to remove him from the class.

Again, I do not write this as a mock on music teachers. I am simply shocked that they don't receive training specific to these students' needs, as they're such a significant part of our public-school population. We're talking about 14% of the American public-school population, and, yet, no one seems to be fazed by this.

Using these experiences as inspiration, I crafted a staff-development workshop on essentially what I've been writing about here. About four years ago, I began going into public-school districts and speaking to their music teachers about using Eurhythmics in the classroom. While my workshop was created to give some insight into special-needs populations and how Eurhythmics could help them, I was soon made more aware of something I wasn't expecting.

The first workshop I presented was in a small public district in New Jersey. I was asked to come in on two mornings to talk to the music teachers from elementary through middle school.

I began by stating the statistics that I mentioned early on—how our schools have become so developmentally, socially, emotionally, and economically diverse. Before I could go on, the teachers began talking to me about how exasperated they were. Far too many shared stories about how one or two students in a single class presented problems that were hard to address. Again, I flashed back to room 2023 in Newark.

Using the 2023 flashback as inspiration, I went off script and told the teachers that story. This presented the perfect path to begin teaching them Eurhythmics techniques and ideas. By the end of the second morning, the teachers were asking me to come back and do more. Again, I heard similar responses: "Why didn't they teach us this in college?" Or "they barely glazed over Eurhythmics in my education courses!"

I also heard from the veteran teachers who have seen the populations in our school shift:

"They never had us back in to explain these populations the way you just did—and I don't understand why."

I was surprised by the reaction to that first workshop. Almost a year later, I received a call from a school district's Supervisor of Humanities. She asked if I would be willing to come in for their staff-development day and speak with all of their teachers— including non-music educators from elementary school through middle school.

I went in for a full day and presented my workshop to various roomfuls of teachers. I was taken aback by how many of them shared stories on how they were overwhelmed with varied learners. When I explained and showed them Eurhythmics techniques, they loved it. Again, the most-often-asked question was: *Why don't they teach us this?*

This trend actually continued. As I mentioned at the start of this book, I was eventually invited to speak at an early-childhood-education conference in Chicago. I presented four workshops in two days to roughly 300 early-childhood educators, and the response was the same I'd been hearing all along. It was—and continues to be—shocking to me.

Please know that the purpose of these stories is not to be an infomercial for my workshops. It is, rather, to show how teachers from preschool to middle school are overwhelmed by the same thing. It's also meant to show the need for this type of training and the benefits it could provide not only to the teachers themselves but also to—most importantly—the students. I have seen it consistently time and time again, and it allowed me to begin to create what I call The New Music Education.

Imagine being a fourth-grade teacher beginning a new school year. In the weeks before school begins, you find out you will have a student in your class who has behavioral and emotional classifications. In a preliminary meeting with the child-study team, you discuss the student's IEP and how it indicates that his social skills would benefit from being surrounded by typical students. You also discuss how he'll have an in-class aide to help him focus on individual work. He will also receive a pull-out once a day, in which he'll get one-on-one reading instruction.

The first day of school comes, and, while the strategies involved with this one student looked great on paper, you find yourself struggling with some of the behaviors this student displays in class. For one thing, he can't sit still. As the first day began, and you were welcoming your students to school, he stood up and began walking around the room. In addition, he was getting in very close on other students' personal space to say hello and ask them (loudly) to be his friend.

While his aide was helping the situation, the student presented a disruption to the rest of the class. Some students were laughing at his behaviors, albeit innocently. A few weeks into school, some students had begun to *imitate* his behaviors. You got frustrated because, instead of the classified student modeling typical students, things have flip-flopped to the other way around.

There were also days when this student came to class and seemed particularly wound up. On these days, he was even louder and more disruptive. There was one girl in your class who was very shy, and when this happened, she got upset. In fact, this girl's mother had emailed you a few times to complain about the situation. There was also a boy in class who was very shy, and when that type of behavior occurred, he actually cried.

You meet with the child-study team to discuss new strategies. A lot of the new ideas proposed seemed good, but then the behaviorist told you it may take a few weeks for the student to adjust. This frustrated you even more. It felt, at times, like this one student was taking up all of your time and energy. You felt an enormous amount of empathy for him, but you also saw what was happening to the other students in class. It was quite overwhelming.

Now imagine this same scenario, but on the first day of school, you were able to call in a specially trained music teacher. She was not designated as the "instrumental" or "general music" teacher, but was almost like a floater. She was available at a moment's notice to come into classrooms and play games, sing songs, or even just play her electric piano quietly while your students work.

In a discussion at staff development the week before school started, you alerted her to the classified student in your class. She took notes and examined the student's IEP. On that first day, she came into your classroom with customized games and activities to help not only this one student but also the others. One game she played involves having the students move and then stop with music. You noticed that she specifically complimented the classified student and reminded him how great a job he was doing. She even told the other students to watch how he does it. She made him a role model.

As the weeks went on, you reached out to the Eurhythmics teacher to talk about how, on certain days, this student came in and was extra wound up. In a subsequent meeting with the Eurhythmics teacher and child-study team, it was decided that on those days, the student would get an extra pull-out and go down to do some one-on-one activities with the Eurhythmics teacher. As this strategy was implemented, you saw an improvement.

Music can, and should be, used in a broader capacity within education. We need to look past the *elective* definition and see it for the powerful force that it is. To quote Dr. Dorita Berger:

"If music is a mirror reflecting . . . life on the planet, then the [Eurhythmics teacher] can reflect and transform [the class] by changing the music, creating new energy vibrations and sensory stimuli, as it were, with interventions that reflect new, modified behavioral alternatives."

She continues:

"Therefore, it is with targeted intent that music can reach beyond aesthetic entertainment to achieve health and well-being. And of course, this implies . . . the interventions of various music features can address specific behavioral treatment goals and objectives."[47]

This is the New Music Education. It is music being used in its fullest capacity. Yes, there is still general music class as well as instrument lessons, band, chorus, and orchestra. Now, however, there's also a Eurhythmics teacher who is available to all staff and students throughout the day.

In fact, as a part of the staff development the week before school started, the Eurhythmics teacher would present a whole-day workshop,

---

47 Berger, pp 99 and 100

in which games, strategies, and techniques are shared and discussed. Included in the workshop were sessions with occupational and speech therapists as well. All teachers and aides in the building now have a basic understanding of Eurhythmics-type strategies and how to use them if need be. Dr. Berger's words regarding this training help to emphasize my point:

"When music fundamentals are . . . experienced and embodied through movement, the body and brain are urged to respond in new ways, influenced by the insistence of forcing function of adequate stimuli and continuous stimulation."[48]

I believe that having non-music educators take a workshop in Eurhythmics will open them up to the dynamic qualities of their own subjects and thus inspire dynamic techniques within those teachers. Teachers now need multiple perspectives from which to address their subjects. To some extent, this has always been the case, but now, it's more so than ever.

I was struck a few years ago by a conversation I was having with two friends of mine. They're a husband and wife, and each holds a PhD: He in biochemistry, and she in organic chemistry. We were having a discussion about why so many students hate math and science. I said, "I think when students walk into a math

---

48 Berger, p 109

or science class, the general tone is *You're never going to be able to understand this*."

I do (honestly) believe that science and math are taught from this perspective. For me (someone who barely graduated high school because of struggles in math) the worst part is, I now have a genuine interest in math and science. It's actually kind of frustrating. I relayed this to my friends, and they both looked at me for a second. Then one spoke up: "Well, science is hard!" I looked at him and responded, "Well, yeah, but so is music." Well, they both burst out laughing!

Once their laughter ended, I said that a non-musician would look at the piano music for a Beethoven sonata and not know what to do with it. But that doesn't mean they still weren't taught to listen to and appreciate it—which many people do. Music is never portrayed or seen as out of reach. I wish math and science were taught more like that. After a pause, they both agreed with me.

Imagine if your math teacher had approached the teaching of math from a more artistic perspective. Thanks to Pythagoras, ancient Greeks actually taught music two ways: As a part of math and also from the more aesthetic perspective as part of drama and poetry class.

We often hear how music is a lot like math. The fact is, it has an extraordinary amount of mathematical attributes. Pythagoras—in addition to creating his famous theorem—also recognized the correlation between the length of strings and the rate at which they vibrate. He subsequently created the whole concept of music theory. The distances between the tones themselves—flats, sharps, and naturals—are referred to as being "whole" and "half" steps. Chords are referenced based on where they sit in numerical order of the scale, or key, they're a part of (a C Major chord in the key of C Major is called the "I chord." D would be the "ii" [lower case because it's minor] and so on). Notes have rhythmic value and are written in beat fractions (quarter notes, half notes, eighth, and sixteenth notes). The spaces between the lines that notes and music are written in are called *measures.*

But we don't (and shouldn't) teach music solely from this perspective. If we did, it would eliminate the aesthetic, expressive, emotional, and social qualities of it. I believe the same can be said about math and science.

Years ago, at a friend's party, I was speaking to a computer programmer. He told me how he didn't think of, or look at, the lines of code he wrote only in the context of mathematical logic. He also saw them as lines of music and visualized them as an artistic picture or painting.

Think about how amazing and wondrous the field of science is, and should be, to young children. Biology is, literally, what children encounter outside while playing. Every little boy and girl are typically, at some point in their young lives, obsessed with bugs and insects. Mud pies, playing in dirt, and eventually playing musical instruments are all scientific investigations of sorts—and they excite children. What happens to that excitement as children progress through school? Are science and math teachers taught to teach their subjects the right way? Just knowing the subject is half the challenge. The ability to teach that subject is something completely different. Imagine if they were taught to teach as an artist. Imagine if all teachers brought a playful and creative tone to their classes.

As student populations have evolved and expanded, what else about education has changed? The biggest change—a new emphasis on students sitting for standardized tests—flies in the face of the developmental diversity that is our public schools. We also cast students into specific roles or identities at earlier and earlier ages—and there's a global emphasis on education as competition. Instead of expanding our ideas to accommodate these incredibly dynamic students, we seem to have done the exact opposite.

Expanding music education and bringing in a Eurhythmics teacher speak to these diverse students. This will help not only students but also the teachers and, perhaps, the school as a whole. These dynamic students cannot be sitting at their desks for hours at a time. To do this doesn't serve the needs of the kids—both those typically developing and those with special needs. Their diagnoses and classifications call for physical movement as well as social and emotional stimulation, and the typically developing kids just need to get up and move.

Imagine a classroom of students who feel confined and pent up. Suddenly the Eurhythmics teacher comes in and plays a quick-reaction game. After that, the class sings a song. Maybe there's an improvisation-based game. The Eurhythmics teacher leaves, and the classroom teacher is now looking at a roomful of aesthetically awake students. The amazing thing is that it took up a mere twenty minutes of the day.

As technology continues to evolve and improve, better therapies and protocols will continue to emerge, which means these populations will continue to expand. This equates to more developmentally diverse and dynamic students who need to develop a healthier sense of self. These students will also create more complex classroom dynamics. This requires creative teachers and programs that can guide these diverse kids through the learning process. Eurhythmics teachers and training can help with this. I know because I've experienced it.

The question of when and how teacher training can and should occur is a constant one. As technology as well as scientific and medical research improve, so must teacher training and know-how. Better, and more thorough, diagnoses mean better understanding and better treatments. And as technology improves, breakthrough research and insight come at greater and greater speeds. Teachers need to be updated on diagnoses, classifications, protocols, and therapies. But when?

I have always felt that the most wasted time of the school year is summer. For eight weeks, a vast majority of America's public-school teachers go off and take a summer job, perhaps doing something that has nothing to do with education. I personally have teacher friends who paint houses, work for catering companies, tend bar, or wait tables. Yes, some teachers work an extended school year or maybe even work at a summer camp, but for the most part, teachers are away from their school and/or district. Why is that?

Think about the opportunity the summer months present not only to learn new teaching techniques but also to study new curricula. Think about it: A full eight weeks to write lesson plans and come up with integrated lessons among other teachers and colleagues. Imagine having eight weeks to take workshops and receive updated training regarding disabilities. Imagine having eight weeks to learn how to teach math, or physics, from multiple perspectives. This is also a great opportunity for teachers to sit together and discuss students.

Imagine, for a minute, you're a third-grade teacher. In the summer months, you would actually sit with the second-grade teachers of the students coming into your class. They could provide insight into learning styles as well as into social and emotional behaviors. Imagine having a week to sit with the second-grade teacher of your classified student (or students) to discuss what strategies worked and which ones didn't work. Having eight uninterrupted weeks to prepare for the school year would be incredible.

Imagine the types of updated technical training that could occur in these eight weeks. I think this question is underlined even more when you consider the sudden crisis in education caused by the COVID-19 pandemic.

In March of 2020, schools across the nation suddenly shuttered, and teachers, students, and their parents were asked to begin teaching and learning through technology. Many teachers as well as entire school districts were forced to learn new technologies on the spot, and many students suffered as a result.

In this book, I've attempted to explain how music affects us not only neurologically but also physically, emotionally, socially, creatively, and intellectually. It's truly aesthetic and dynamic which makes using it in more expanded ways perfect for today's developmentally diverse classrooms. I hope the experiences I've shared helped to get my point across.

I believe that having a Eurhythmics teacher in our schools would be an invaluable resource. It is something that I see as a benefit for not only the students but also for the teachers, administrators, and school as a whole.

I also believe that we need to view our teachers more on the plane of creative individuals. Teachers should be seen as artists—because they are. I also believe a teaching degree should be awarded as a Bachelor of Fine Arts degree. Modern-day teachers are required to do more than spew information. They need to understand a sensory diagnosis; be aware of problems at home; understand the complications of anxiety, depression, and ADHD; make sure students are not being bullied—in the classroom and/or online; make sure all of the kids are safe during a lockdown drill; and be able to seamlessly pivot to online virtual learning when a global pandemic hits. And, as COVID-19 showed us they also need to be able to move to a completely different platform and teach in a way they never imagined.[49]

---

49 I actually believe that if teaching degrees were awarded as BFAs and MFAs, it would change the mindset of teachers. They would view themselves more as creative individuals and approach their work more from that perspective. This, I believe, would have helped significantly with the transition from live to virtual education in the midst of the pandemic. As a Boston-based Dalcroze teacher responded when asked how her live/virtual transition went: "It wasn't a problem. I had to improvise and make stuff up . . . that's what [Dalcroze teachers] are trained to do."

Education has changed exponentially, and we need to realize that it has made the job of teaching incredibly dynamic. I would think an investment like this wouldn't be seen as absurd. After all, our children are the future. Imagine what the world is going to look like in ten year's time? Are we preparing our kids for it? Are we preparing our teachers for it?

7
EPILOGUE

I began writing this book in 2014. It is truly a labor of passion but also one of adjustment and updating.

As I was getting ready to (finally) submit my manuscript, the COVID-19 pandemic hit. Society was thrown into chaos as American schools—both public and private—were shuttered en masse. Suddenly, every aspect of schooling was shifted to tech-based online and/or virtual learning. Teachers who had no idea what Zoom or Google Hangouts were found themselves thrown into a platform they not only had to learn to operate but also how to teach effectively with and through it.

The whole idea of "school" was thrown into disarray. Students, and teachers, were ripped from the daily routine and construct that is "school". Every aspect from class schedules, seeing friends, how and what to study, to graduations and proms was wrecked. It was overwhelming from every imaginable perspective.

Districts were suddenly faced with students who didn't have home computers or tablets. There were students who lacked fast and/or reliable Internet connections. It was a disaster. America was suddenly overwhelmed by the dynamic and complex ecosystem that is education. In the early days of the pandemic and repeated attempts to adapt to online/virtual learning—as well as everything else—the state of Virginia threw their hands up and flat-out cancelled the rest of the schoolyear in April.

America was also collectively aghast at the extraordinary number of students who go to school every day and qualify for free breakfast and lunch. With schools shuttered, the curtain was lifted, and the country was introduced to the massive population of kids who see the main function of school as a foodbank.

Special education, and all of its services, was severely affected. How were kids going to get OT, speech, and/or social-skills classes? Students with special needs, who thrive on the consistency and services of school, were completely removed from all of it.

COVID-19 cast a whole new light on not only how students learn but also on the fact that "school" is more than the place kids go to learn math and science. It's is also where lifelong friendships are formed, and is also where many students get the structure and discipline they need and crave.

What was going to happen with all of this, literally, disappearing overnight?

Were the teachers themselves prepared for such a massive shift? Were they able to pivot and adapt? Had they themselves been taught properly for something so sudden and significant?

By early June of 2020, a significant number of American schools had ended their year. That meant that by mid-June administrators, teachers, superintendents, and parents had about 11 weeks to sit down and begin discussing possible scenarios for the 2020–2021 schoolyear. Despite the fact that most schools were shut down by the beginning of April, there was no national strategy put in place. There were no creative ideas or solutions discussed, no national panel on education to "table top" scenarios and come up with creative and/ or dynamic strategies.

As the 2020/2021 schoolyear began, a vast majority of public school districts did so remotely. Again, it varied from state to state as well as town to town. My hometown school district went back to in-person instruction in the fall. But the town next to ours still had their students attending remotely. My hometown school district (despite going back to in-person instruction) has switched to full remote, back to in-person, and back to remote so many times, the kids have whiplash.

As the vaccines rolled out and things have begun improving, I hope that we begin thinking about the fall. As the 2021–2022 schoolyear begins, the pandemic's lingering effects will be far from over. Are districts properly preparing to educate children who will be walking back into a building after being out of it for more than a year? How are these kids going to be taught?

Rates of anxiety and depression amongst children were high before COVID-19. Are we making plans for a collective national student body that will be walking back into the routine of school having experienced some aspect of this global pandemic? Maybe a parent or family member passed away. Maybe a parent (or parents) lost their job. Even if none of these things have happened, students will be coming back to school having lived through what truly is a global humanitarian crisis.

A study released in October, 2020 by Columbia University showed the number of Americans living in poverty had grown by 8 million. That equates to more children coming to school living through the effects of economic distress. We can't go into the next schoolyear believing that kids will walk into their school buildings and just pick up where they left off. There will be students coming to school who are not just behind academically, but socially, and emotionally as well. Every piece of the education ecosystem has been impacted by this moment and we need to put plans and protocols in place for the start of the schoolyear.

We are in the midst of an extraordinary moment in history. The COVID-19 pandemic will have a lasting impact on all of us, especially our children. Included in the daily routine of school should be the opportunity for our kids to express themselves—and this should be the case for the unforeseeable future.

In 1958, the scholar Viktor Lowenfeld wrote about how important it is for children to express themselves artistically. He believed the post-World War I German schools prevented their children from properly expressing the crisis they'd just experienced, and what they had just lived through. Lowenfeld also believed this repression is what led to a rise of aggression, frustration, an increased national anger, and eventually World War II. In his book *Creative and Mental Growth* he wrote:

"The child who uses creative activity as an emotional outlet will gain freedom and flexibility as a result of the release of unnecessary tensions. However, the child who feels frustrated develops inhibitions and, as a result, will feel restricted in his personality. The child who has developed freedom and flexibility in his expression will be able to face new situations without difficulties. Through his flexible approaches toward the expression of his own ideas, he will not only face new situations properly but will adjust himself to them easily. The inhibited and restricted child, accustomed to imitating rather than expressing himself creatively, will prefer to go along with set patterns in life. He will not be able to

adjust to new situations quickly but will rather try to lean upon others as the easiest way out. Since it is generally accepted that progress, success, and happiness in life depend greatly upon the ability to adjust to new situations, the importance of art education for personality growth and development can easily be recognized." (Lowenfeld, p 7)

I have friends with children ranging in age from elementary to high school, and they have all expressed concern over their children's mental state. One parent recently told me how his high school aged son went for his yearly physical exam and spent most of the visit telling his doctor how stressed out he was over the pandemic. Are these things being considered both within the context of COVID and "post-COVID" school?

I believe when school resumes to a full in-person model, it should include Eurhythmics classes for all students. This would be enormously beneficial. Students will be coming into school carrying things other than backpacks. The will bring unique experiences, and emotions, related to living through a global humanitarian crisis. We need to provide ways for our kids to work through this extraordinary moment. Eurhythmics can help with that. It is, after all, a method of teaching that stresses the importance of feeling oneself move within the context of a group. The reinforcing of time, space, and energy concepts will be extraordinarily helpful to a collective student body who have been in and out of their school building in a tumultuous year. My fear is that school doors will open for the 2021–2022 schoolyear and we will try and hit the ground running as if nothing happened. This would be detrimental.

In addition to the effects of COVID-19, technology has continued to change drastically. As technology evolves, how will childhood development continue to be affected? When you consider what is already happening, the thought is pretty daunting. Technology has infiltrated every aspect of our lives—in both good and bad ways. Yes, it enabled elements of the economy to thrive by allowing people to work from home. It played a massive role in the development of the COVID vaccines. It gives us access to information as well as to our work colleagues, family, and friends. But it also continues to drive wedges between us.

Social media has had a profound effect on the concept and idea of truth. In addition to providing amazing benefits, it also provides a way to spread massive amounts of lies, rumors, and disinformation. Some academics and sociologists believe it's changing the way we think as well as process information and is also having an effect on the way our children develop.

The great musician and music producer T-Bone Burnett had a thought regarding this:

"Technology does only one thing—it tends toward efficiency. It has no ethics. Its code is binary. But everything that's interesting in life—everything that makes life worth living—happens between the binary. Mercy is not binary. Love is not binary. Music and art are not binary. You and I are not binary."[50]

50 T Bone Burnett keynote address, Americana Music Festival & Conference, Thursday, September 22, 2016

The continued evolution of technology also means academic, scientific, and medical theories, tests, and ideas are going to arrive faster and in the form of treatments, medications, and therapies. In essence, life is going to speed up even more, meaning that school populations are going to constantly evolve as well. This means districts are going to have to change and adapt yet again—and it's going to happen sooner than anyone expects.

We are in the midst of nothing short of a technical, as well as public-health, revolution, and every aspect of life has been affected. Consider just the emotional impact social media and COVID-19 have had on the development of our kids. We are just seeing the front end of the social media/tech aspect alone—COVID-19 has only added to an already complex situation.

The other thing that shocked me was the complete lack of creativity and/or ingenuity when it came to re-opening schools in the fall of 2020. There were no cohesive strategies or protocols discussed. Instead of gathering a committee of educators, administrators, thinkers, educational philosophers, artists, designers, sociologists, and child psychologists—we kind of collectively crossed our fingers. Could teachers and staff trained in a creative approach like Eurhythmics have been able to pivot into a moment like a global pandemic more seamlessly and with more ideas?

As I said at the very beginning of this book: Teaching is a dynamic and creative profession, as is the whole of education. But when it came time to address how we were going to adapt to this extraordinary moment, there was no creativity or dynamic ideas.

Districts were scrambling to come up with viable strategies to accommodate things like better ventilation in buildings and other safety measures. Districts were also faced with the backwards task of creating *more* physical space in schools to accommodate *fewer* students as to adjust for social distancing. In New York City three weeks before schools were set to open, the discovery was made that there were a significant number of public schools whose windows couldn't open. Other districts had students return with no protocols or plans in place and, within days, or weeks, had to shut down again.

Was the lack of creative ideas because most teachers are not trained to be creative? I'm asking this question because if the pandemic is an example of the types of changes we are going to be experiencing, rethinking the way all teachers are trained is an important consideration. This pandemic is an extraordinary moment that requires extraordinary, outside-the-box, dynamic, and creative solutions. This, again, proves that dynamic training like Dalcroze Eurhythmics will help all teachers—not just those who teach music—adapt and be able to come up with ways to adjust to moments like this. I also believe it will enhance their use of technology and online virtual learning.

Are we ready for these constant shifts? Are our teachers being trained to be dynamic, flexible, and creative in classrooms that will keep changing socially, emotionally, developmentally, cognitively, physically, and intellectually? Are our school buildings themselves ready for this? How about the administrations overseeing them?

In the time since I began writing this book, much has continued to change around me (and you) technologically—and also from public-health as well as environmental standpoints.

The number of students attending public schools who are anxious and/or depressed continues to rise. I had to adjust my statistical numbers more than once on those specific populations during the writing process. The students attending our schools continue to be more dynamic and bring more specific needs to the classroom.

In addition to a global pandemic, wildfires, floods, and hurricanes, and things like opioid crises continue to devastate entire towns—including their schools. How are those administrations and teachers responding? Are there creative strategies in place to accommodate such a situation?

In June of 2018, the results of a massive study meant to improve teacher effectiveness were published. This effort was undertaken by the Bill and Melinda Gates Foundation at a cost of $575 million. An article in *Education Week* said the project ". . . largely fell short . . ." of its aim to improve the achievement of poor and minority students. One of the lead researchers in the project was quoted in *Education Week* specifically on how the project was focused on a singular aspect:

"This suggests that focusing on [teacher effectiveness]
alone is not likely to be the potent sort of intervention
that really moves student outcomes . . ."

He then went on to say that a more dynamic approach is needed, and perhaps consideration needs to be taken toward other factors more closely aligned with children themselves. The factors mentioned include nutrition, home life, and social and emotional aspects of childhood. In other words, these are factors that are a part of a larger education ecosystem—factors that were exposed in the midst of the pandemic.

When I read the Gates report, I was not surprised by those conclusions. In fact, I was encouraged by the willingness of those affiliated with the project to admit that education cannot be boiled down to a singular element. It is many things working together and singularly at the same time. It is an ecosystem, and it is one that is delicate and dynamic. It has an extraordinary number of parts that are all intertwined and dependent on each other.

The children coming into the school depend on the community that surrounds it. Is it economically, socially, civically, and domestically sound? In other words, is the community functional? Are the parents responsible? Is there accessibility to healthy food?

Is the school building itself sound? Do the toilets flush? Are the ceilings leaking? Is there mold? Do the water fountains work? If so, is the water safe to drink? Does the cafeteria serve healthy food? Is the school clean? Do all the lights work? How many books does the library have? How about the principal? Does she/he understand the community around the school? Can she relate to the parents and the children? How about the teachers? Are they competent—and not just in their subjects? Do they understand the children of the community? Do they understand their needs?

If one piece of the ecosystem isn't working or is working poorly, it falls onto the others to support it. If multiple pieces are failing, the others feel a greater weight. If that weight gets too heavy, the system collapses. Mind you, I say this as someone who worked in a school that did collapse. It was an awful experience that taught me how delicate and dynamic the education ecosystem really is.

This delicate ecosystem is not limited to urban or rural districts. As we are now seeing, seemingly wealthy suburban school districts are suddenly experiencing increased rates of depression and anxiety. Students there, in addition to hours of homework, also feel crazy pressure to "succeed" at an absurd level.

There's also been an enormous number of children affected by the opioid epidemic. These children have not only been born to opioid-addicted parents but now also suffer undiagnosed mental conditions. Maybe a parent (or parents) are incarcerated as a result.

Added to all of this is the political divisiveness that has engulfed our society. A recent CDC study cited how the polarized political climate—in addition to poverty and social-media pressure—that is adding stress to the already delicate world of being a teenager. We clearly have some things we need to work through.

The shifts affecting education and childhood development that I've been speaking about can inspire change. In fact, these things inspired a South Carolina school district to do something some would view as radical: Change their public schools to Montessori schools—and these are not limited to early-childhood centers or preschools. It was a decision that arose out of necessity, and the results have been pretty amazing.

Latta Elementary School is located in a rural area of South Carolina and serves grades Pre-K to four. Seventy percent of the school's students qualify for reduced-price or free lunch, and a little less than half are students of color. District Superintendent Dr. John Kirby took a look at the students of Latta and wondered if they were being educated the right way. Was he serving his students' needs?

He took a step back and examined his students' well-being as well as academic performance, and it inspired him to make Latta a Montessori school. Kirby recognized how Montessori's emphasis on social and emotional development could better serve his students. This transition required him to speak directly with his teachers and not only have them agree to the change but also undergo the training needed to become Montessori teachers. The process took five years and had teachers taking summer as well as evening courses. Some teachers were thirty-year veterans but made the shift, and the benefits have been tremendous.

Latta's fourth-grade state math test scores were 21% higher than their traditional public-school counterparts. Their third-grade English/Language Arts state test scores were 38% higher than those of traditional public-school students.

But it's not just about the test scores.

Through Montessori, the students at Latta have also learned about self-agency and autonomy. The use of tactile-based learning activities encourages group work and also helps with sensory components of learning. In addition, students' understanding of their relationship to the environment is a key component of Montessori education. It all helps with the development of the whole child. In addition to all of the above, student classroom behavior has improved.

Finally, Montessori is also dependent on parental involvement. Dr. Kirby had to not only get his teachers and staff to agree to the change, but the parents as well. In other words, this change is one that engaged the entire ecosystem that is education. A shift was made—and not just to benefit the students. It was done to benefit the community.

Latta School in South Carolina is one example of the types of changes needed regarding the education of our children. It takes the willingness of administrators, teachers, and the community to look at what they could do to best serve their students and then implement those policies or strategies.

Information like this, and all of my continued work and research, is what this book is truly about. I do not believe that Eurhythmics, and music, can singularly—by themselves—improve American public education. What I do believe is expanding music education through Eurhythmics can add an important piece to an already delicate system and provide more support that will ultimately help our kids to discover who they are and how they can be a unique part of the community around them.

After all, that's what education is truly about.

I would like to end with a quote from Dalcroze himself regarding teacher training and the future:

"The only living art is that which grows out of one's own experiences. It is just the same with teaching; it is quite impossible to develop others until one has [proven] one's own powers in every direction, until one has learnt to conquer oneself, to make oneself better, to suppress bad tendencies, to strengthen good ones, and, in the place of the primitive being, to make one more complete who, having consciously formed himself, knows his powers...I consider that one does not require to be a genius in order to teach others, but that one certainly does require strong conviction, enthusiasm, persistence, and joy in life. All these qualities are equally derived from the control and knowledge of the self."

The "knowledge of the self" Dalcroze speaks of is that of self-discovery. This is the purpose of education for not only the students but the teachers as well. Eurhythmics can be a valuable asset in that journey. I believe the time to make that happen is now.

WORKS CITED

Berger, Dorita S. *Eurhythmics for Autism and Other Neurophysiologic Diagnoses A Sensorimotor Music-Based Treatment Approach.* Jessica Kingsley Publishers, 2016

Dalcroze, Emile Jaques. *Rhythm, Music and Education.* G.P. Putnam's Sons, 1921

Dalcroze, Emile Jaques and John W. Harvey. *The Eurhythmics of Jaques-Dalcroze.* Wildside Press, 2007

Langer, Susanne K: *Philosophy in a New Key: A Study in the Symbolism of Reason, Rite, and Art.* Harvard College, 1982

Levitin, Daniel. *This Is Your Brain on Music: The Science of a Human Obsession.* Dutton, 2006

Lowenfeld, Viktor. *Creative and Mental Growth: A Textbook on Art Education.* Macmillan Co., 1947

Schneck, Daniel J. and Berger, Dorita S. *The Music Effect: Music Physiology and Clinical Applications.* Jessica Kingsley Publishers, 2006

BIBLIOGRAPHY

While the aforementioned cited works played a significant role in my research, the works below added to that knowledge. I included them as a guide for anyone interested in pursuing and/or seeing how I was inspired by these authors and thinkers.

Auster Paul. *Winter Journal.* Henry Holt and Company, LLC, 2012

Byrne, David. *Arboretum.* Canongate Books Ltd., 2006, 2019

Byrne, David. *How Music Works.* McSweenys San Francisco, 2012, 2013

Carr, Nicholas. *The Shallows: What the Internet is Doing to Our Brains.* W.W. Norton & Company, In., New York, NY 2010, 2011, 2020

Choksy, Lois and Abramson, Robert and Gillespie, Avon and Woods, David. *Teaching Music in the Twentieth Century.* Prentice-Hall, 1986

Dewey, John. *Art as Experience.* the Penguin Group, 1934

Dewey, John. *How to Think.* Dover Publications, 1997

Eisner, Elliot W. *The Arts and the Creation of Mind.* Yale University Press, 2002

Hirsch, E.D, Jr. *The Making of Americans: Democracy and Our Schools.* Yale University Press, 2009

Louv, Richard. *Last Child in the Woods: Saving Our Children From Nature Deficit Disorder.* Algonquin Books of Chapel Hill 2005

Mannes, Elena. *The Power of Music: Pioneering Discoveries in the New Science of Song .* Walter & Company N.Y., 2011

Mead, Virginia Hoge. *Dalcroze Eurhythmics in Today's Music Classroom.* Kent State University, 1994

McCredie, Scott. *Balance: In Search of the Lost Sense.* Little Brown and Company, 2007

Ravitch, Diane. *The Death and Life of the Great American School System: How Testing and Choice Are Undermining Education.* Basic Books, 2010

Sacks, Oliver. *Musicophilia: Tales of Music and the Brain.* Alfred A. Knopf, N.Y., Toronto, 2007

Schwab, Klaus. *The Fourth Industrial Revolution.* Crown Business N.Y., 2016

Spector, Irwin. *Rhythm and Life: The Work of Emile Jaques-Dalcroze.* Pendragon Press Stuyvesant, N.Y., 1990

Westney, William. *The Perfect Wrong Note: Learning to Trust Your Musical Self.* Amadeus Press, 2003

Wooden, John. *My Personal Best Life Lessons from an All-American Journey.* McGraw Hill, 2004

ABOUT THE AUTHOR

Patrick Cerria is a New Jersey based musician, educator, and Dalcroze Eurhythmics teacher. He earned the Dalcroze Elementary Certificate from The Juilliard Dalcroze School in 2007 and has spent the last 14 years teaching and working with varied populations of students. Patrick is currently working towards his Dalcroze License at the Marta Sanchez Dalcroze Training Center at Carnegie Mellon University in Pittsburgh.

When not teaching, playing, writing, researching, reading about, or listening to music, Patrick spends time with his wife, two children, and their dog. In addition to his continued studies in Eurhythmics, he is currently attempting to learn the game of golf.

In 2020, Patrick and his wife Laura founded the 501 c3 company Education Flow. Through Education Flow he hopes to gain funding to further studies specific to the expansion of music education as well as Dalcroze Eurhythmics. *Finding the Flow* is his first book.

Made in the USA
Middletown, DE
07 November 2021